Llewellyn's
2012
Witches'
Companion

An Almanac for Everyday Living

Llewellyn's 2012 Witches' Companion

ISBN 978-0-7387-1211-6

Cover art © Tim Foley
Cover designer: Lynne Menturweck
Designer: Joanna Willis
Art Director: Lynne Menturweck
Editor: Nicole Edman

Interior illustrations: Kathleen Edwards: 12, 14, 17, 20, 58, 61, 103, 107, 112, 153, 157, 197, 201; Tim Foley: 9, 33, 34, 35, 65, 79, 81, 83, 123, 133, 137, 171, 177, 185, 207, 208, 211; Bri Hermanson: 48, 51, 54, 92, 96, 98, 141, 144, 147, 188, 190, 193, 238, 242, 244; Christa Marquez: 25, 28, 70, 75, 114, 116, 119, 163, 165, 227, 229, 230, 233; Rik Olson: 38, 41, 44, 86, 89, 125, 127, 129, 181, 215, 217, 220.

Additional illustrations: Llewellyn Art Department

Any Internet references contained in this work are current at publication time, but the publisher cannot guarantee that a specific location will continue to be maintained.

You can order Llewellyn annuals and books from *New Worlds*, Llewellyn's magazine catalog. To request a free copy of the catalog, call toll-free 1-877-NEW-WRLD, or visit our Web site at http://www.llewellyn.com.

Printed in the United States of America.

Llewellyn Worldwide Ltd.
2143 Wooddale Drive
Woodbury, MN 55125-2989
www.llewellyn.com

Contents

Witchy Living • 65

Day-by-Day Witchcraft

Witchcraft Essentials • 123

Practices, Rituals & Spells

Magical Transformations · 185

Everything Old Is New Again

Community Forum

PROVOCATIVE OPINIONS ON CONTEMPORARY TOPICS

Cannabis and the Environment

Melanie Marquis

It can end world hunger, clean the air, reduce pollution, restore depleted soils, and save forests. It provides a quickly renewable source of fiber, fuel, energy, and complete nutrition, and it can grow nearly any place on Earth. Talk about a magickal plant! Cannabis, considered sacred by many witches for its value in spellcraft and ritual, can also play a major role in healing the planet. As more and more localities around the globe welcome the growing and use of cannabis, it's time to take another look at the environmental (and magickal) benefits of the herb we call Herb.

An Herb Most Magickal

As one of humankind's first domesticated crops, cannabis has helped man survive and thrive for thousands of years. Cannabis cultivation began in China around 8000 BCE and spread to surrounding regions. It became a common crop throughout Asia, used for fiber, oil, food, medicine, and ritual. In Japan, cannabis was an early and important element of the native religion of Shinto, where it was considered sacred to the solar goddess Amaterasu and used also for purification, banishing, and summoning spirits of the dead. Cannabis made its way to England around AD 70, and by the sixteenth century, cannabis crops dotted the landscape in Russia, North America, and Europe. Early American colonists grew hemp for its useful fiber. It has been regarded as one of Earth's most useful and sacred plants for thousands of years. Yet today, cannabis is regulated by law, and permits to grow it are difficult or impossible to come by in many places around the world.

But times are changing, and cannabis is making a comeback as governments and populations conclude that the benefits of this plant far outweigh objections. As we observe more and more effects of man's greed and devastation of the environment, we come to reject the current order and open our minds to other possibilities. Cannabis offers a key to a greener and friendlier planet, capable of repairing man's relationship with the natural world. As witches, we specialize in independent thinking—decide for yourself what you think about the cannabis plant, then let your voice be heard.

What's In a Name?

Hemp, cannabis, marijuana—what's the difference? The distinctions can be confusing but are nonetheless important to understand due to governmental restrictions pertaining to

various classifications of the herb. Marijuana (which is psychoactive) and hemp (which is not) share the scientific name, *Cannabis sativa*. Strains of cannabis are custom-bred into either marijuana for recreational or medicinal use, or into hemp for industrial or nutritional use. Although hemp won't get anyone stoned, looks distinctly different, and would be avoided like the plague by any serious marijuana grower (placing marijuana plants near a hemp crop would yield very seedy buds), many governments fail to make exceptions for hemp in their anti-marijuana provisions, classifying both hemp and marijuana as cannabis, thereby shutting down what could otherwise be an incredibly profitable industry.

Marijuana (which is psychoactive) and hemp (which is not) share the scientific name, *Cannabis sativa*.

Was it an accident or simple oversight that allowed industrial hemp to be demonized along with its high-inducing sister? Hemp had, after all, been in use for thousands of years without stirring up a fuss. So what happened?

In the United States, hemp cultivation was an active and promising industry until 1937, when the Marijuana Tax Act was passed, imposing a hefty tax on hemp, which made it less profitable to produce. This move coincided with the rise of timber and oil interests, companies whose products directly competed with the more environmentally friendly and (previously) cheaper-to-produce hemp products. Economic giants—including William Randolph Hearst, who owned a thriving timber business, and DuPont, which procured patents in 1937 for making plastics from petroleum and coal—engaged in a propaganda campaign against the evils of "marijuana," a term not commonly known at the time.

Advocates for the hemp industry are therefore adamant about drawing clear lines between high-inducing marijuana and industrial hemp, asserting that hemp and marijuana are entirely different plants. Personally, I find no reason to draw distinctions; I feel that advocates on every side of the marijuana and/or hemp legalization movement could better accomplish their aims by working together. People today can understand that just as other crops can be bred into certain varieties with particular characteristics, the versatile cannabis plant can be bred in a multitude of ways for a multitude

of purposes. The fact that certain varieties of it can catch someone a buzz should not overshadow cannabis' greater applications in providing for the needs of humans while healing the planet.

Weed Can Feed

Hunger and malnutrition still plague humans, and cannabis could provide the cure. Growing in nearly any weather, thriving in poor soil conditions, reaching full maturity in only 120 days, and naturally resistant to weeds, diseases, and pests, cannabis gardens could provide a renewable, high-yield food source in barren areas where good soil and precipitation are scarce. One tiny cannabis seed contains 25–35 percent protein, and just a handful of these little beauties a day is enough to sustain an average adult. Second only to soy in protein content and easier to digest, this botanical has even been called a super food, as it is the only single food source that supplies all of man's daily nutritional requirements necessary for survival.

Cannabis seeds contain all twenty-one known amino acids, which are often described as the building blocks of protein. Amino acids provide energy and are vital to the maintenance and repair of tissues, muscles, bones, hair, and skin. They're also essential to the production of neurotransmitters, enzymes, body fluids, and certain hormones. In addition to its amazing mix of amino acids, cannabis is also the only food to contain all the essential fatty acids, which are vital for proper body functioning and growth. In fact, cannabis ranks highest among all plants in its total essential fatty acid content, and it's one of the few foods to contain the perfect balance of Omega-6 and Omega-3 fatty acids, the 3:1 ratio most recommended by nutritionists and health experts.

The cannabis plant is not only nutritious, but versatile. The seeds can be made into cooking oil; added to foods such as pastas, rice, soups, and salads; ground into flour; or eaten straight, hulled and perhaps lightly toasted. The seeds can even be made into vitamin rich, easily digestible hemp milk and ice cream products.

Cannabis leaves and buds are also edible, and the plant can be bred to either minimize or maximize THC content. The leaves and buds from plants grown to minimize THC can be used fresh or cooked like other vegetables, offering a ready source of vitamin A that won't get you high, while food cooked with cannabis grown to maximize THC offers an herbal relief for many ailments. In impoverished areas where pharmaceuticals are often hard to come by, marijuana offers promise as a medicine that could be locally grown and obtained at little or no cost.

Cannabis grows quickly in nearly any climate and any soil, and it's one of the healthiest foods on the planet. Producing a foot-long taproot in only thirty days, the plant prevents topsoil erosion and actually leaves the soil in better condition, making it useful in helping restore over-grazed areas and depleted farmlands. Self-sufficient, renewable cannabis farms could provide many impoverished communities with a reliable, renewable source of complete nutrition. If there is really such a thing as a single loaf that can feed the multitudes, that loaf is most certainly made of miraculous cannabis.

Keep the Trees, Use the Hemp

Trees provide beauty, shade, oxygen, and wildlife habitat, often growing for hundreds of years before being chopped down in seconds to be processed into paper, furniture, and other necessities. As witches, it's important to us to protect and conserve what's left of the world's forests, and hemp offers a way to do just that. Whereas an average acre of forest yields less than two tons of fiber and takes years to grow, an acre of hemp can yield up to eight tons of fiber and matures in only four months, quickly leaving the land ready and in good condition for the next planting. This fiber can be made into a pulp that outperforms wood-based paper while being more environmentally sound and less costly to produce. Hemp-based paper lasts longer and is much stronger than paper made from tree pulp. In fact, the oldest surviving piece of paper is a Chinese relic made of hemp and mulberry dating from around 100 BCE. Because of its natural brightness, hemp paper can be bleached using hydrogen peroxide. This is a simpler, cheaper, more environmentally sound method than bleaching with the toxic chemicals required in tree-based paper manufacturing, so it saves costs while reducing pollution.

Hemp is a highly viable, renewable, and recyclable paper source, growing much more quickly and able to withstand many more trips through the recycling process than wood paper. As current paper-manufacturing equipment can make paper from hemp pulp just as well as from tree pulp, reducing deforestation in favor of hemp cultivation would be a smooth and cost-effective transition. Why waste irreplaceable trees to satisfy our paper needs when hemp can do the

job better? Hemp paper was good enough to record the Declaration of Independence and the U.S. Constitution—isn't it good enough to take into the bathroom or host the morning news?

Putting King Cotton's Pollution In Its Place

Put simply, cotton is not very ecologically (or economically) sensible. Heavily taxing to the land on which it grows, this "King of Crops" causes erosion, mineral depletion, and toxicity. Cannabis, however, leaves the dirt aerated, in place, chemical-free, and stocked with nutrients. Unlike cannabis, which is naturally resistant to pests, weeds, and disease, cotton is highly prone to such menaces and requires a large quantity of costly, often toxic pesticides, herbicides, and fertilizers in order to thrive. Although it comprises only 2.5 percent of the world's farmland, cotton crops use 16 percent of the world's insecticides.* These toxins seep into soil and contaminate waterways. Cotton is also more susceptible to drought than is the hardy hemp plant, with a single dry season capable of wiping out entire cotton crops.

With just one acre of hemp producing as much viable fiber for textiles as two to three acres of cotton, farmers could get greater value from less land, maximizing profits. As for quality, cotton just doesn't cut it. Cannabis is three times stronger and is more durable, breathable, and flame retardant; from a magickal perspective, the mystical energies inherent in hemp cloth make it ideal for ritual wear. Instead of letting pesticides pollute the planet and allowing cotton to devastate the land, we could be making our clothing and other textiles in a much greener fashion and healing the land at the same time with good, green hemp.

Biodegradable Pot Plastics

It's true: the mighty herb can even be used to fashion high-quality, non-toxic, biodegradable plastic products of virtually any shape. Most plastic is made from cellulose, typically derived from petroleum through a difficult and highly polluting process. Such petroleum-based plastic does not degrade easily and can stay in our landfills for years. But petroleum isn't the only source of cellulose; the substance is also found in plants, and cannabis produces more of it than any other botanical. Hemp can be made into toys, dishes, soda bottles, CD cases, packing materials, cellophane, insulation, and even car bodies. Used today in the manufacturing of door panels and other components by several European carmakers, hemp-based plastic is stronger than steel.

---

*EJF. 2007. *The Deadly Chemicals in Cotton*. Environmental Justice Foundation in collaboration with Pesticide Action Network. U.K. London. ISBN 1-904523-10-2.

This isn't new technology. In 1941, Henry Ford demonstrated that his car built from hemp-based plastic could withstand many more blows from a sledgehammer without denting than could a steel-bodied car. Cars made with the built-in benefits of cannabis are less likely to be crushed in an accident, and they also weigh less, resulting in significantly better fuel economy.

For the magickal community, cannabis plastics bring advancements. The incenses, essential oils, and loose herbs we buy for use in magick could be packaged in eco-friendly, biodegradable bags and bottles made of hemp-based plastic, better preserving and even boosting the magickal power of the product. Instead of cutting down trees to make tarot cards, altars, and incense burners, why not make those products out of fast-growing, truly renewable hemp?

As our dumps steadily fill up with refuse that will last many lifetimes, we look for alternatives that are kinder to the earth, and products that leave a minimal impact on the planet. Biodegradable, recyclable pot plastics fit the mold.

Better Biofuel

With carbon emissions from gasoline- and diesel-powered vehicles doing their share in overheating the atmosphere and keeping our skies smog-filled, cleaner burning biofuels have become the solution for a growing number of drivers. Carbon monoxide emissions from standard diesel are 47 percent higher than carbon monoxide emissions from biodiesel, a fuel created from heated plant parts called biomass. With hemp growing to heights of 15 feet in seventy to ninety days, it's the world's top producer of biomass, capable of yielding up to ten tons per acre in only a few short months. Using the hemp plant as a biofuel creates a closed carbon cycle, as the plants absorb as much carbon dioxide while living as they release when burned, an effect that offers hope to a planet facing the formidable challenge of reducing the impact of global warming.

Another advantage of hemp biodiesel becomes clear in the face of a crisis such as the 2010 BP oil spill. If a similar amount of pure hemp biodiesel had made its way into water, over 85 percent of the fuel would have fully degraded naturally in just twenty-eight days.

Hemp is a traditional ingredient in the witch's broom, but it can power our everyday, non-magickal vehicles in a way that doesn't hurt Mother Earth.

Cannabis Cities?

As witches in tune with nature, it can be a bit depressing to contemplate the sheer volume of concrete that is plastered on our planet. Good for skateboarding, yes, but that concrete tends to leave scars on the environment that stick around long after the skateboarders are harassed by the police and sent home. Traditional concrete can emit low-level radiation for generations after its original manufacturing, and the amount of sand, rock, and toxic coal byproducts required to make traditional concrete is remarkable. In comparison, concrete and other building materials made from cannabis are safer and are derived from a renewable, sustainable resource.

Hemp can be made into virtually any building material, from concrete and insulation to pipes, plywood, paint, and stucco. Hemp-made homes are energy-efficient and durable while minimizing the need for more environmentally taxing and toxic materials. Buildings utilizing hemp materials in the walls and structure have a natural elasticity that may be especially well-suited for areas prone to earthquakes; instead of breaking or cracking, a hemp-made structure is more likely to sway and flex when the ground shakes.

There is also the magickal benefit to consider. As a witch, do you feel that living in an environmentally friendly, hemp-made home would support your magickal and psychic powers better than would a house made of polluting products derived by ravaging the environment? What benefits would you enjoy? What, if any, would be the drawbacks? Building our cities out of cannabis might seem like a pipe dream, but it's a pipe dream well worth pursuing.

Cannabis and the Sun

Could cannabis help humans combat negative health effects caused by ozone depletion? Some theorists say yes, linking the effects commonly caused by UVB radiation sickness to benefits shown in many people who take cannabis medicinally. An interesting feature of the cannabis plant is that the more UVB radiation it receives, the more THC it produces, and according to Alan Gordon, founder of the American Drug History Institute (and holder of a degree in Drug Policy, Hemp, and the Environment from Pennsylvania State University), THC provides the human body with relief from UVB radiation sickness symptoms and offers future protection against the sun's most damaging rays. Further research may lead to valuable discoveries.

. . . .

Providing fiber, fuel, food, and medicine, and containing a tremendous amount of inherent magickal power, cannabis is one of the most useful plants on Earth, and it's a key to healing the planet. As witches, we are stewards of nature, and if we really want to, we have the power to change the world.

RESOURCES, Accessed August 2010

Benhaim, Paul. "Hemp Plastics Show Their Mettle." Hemphasis. http://www.hemphasis.net/Building/plasticmettle.htm.

Hemphasis. "Chronology of Hemp Throughout History." http://www.hemphasis.net/History/history.htm.

Briggs, Jeremy. "Hemp: A Complete Food." Hemphasis. http://www.hemphasis.net/Nutrition/nutrition.htm.

Body Ecology. "Hemp: Is This Nutty Food Source Good for You?" http://www.bodyecology.com/08/04/10/hemp_nutty_food_source_good_for_you.php.

North American Industrial Hemp Council. "Hemp Facts." http://www.naihc.org/hemp-information/286-hemp-facts.

Soiferman, Ezra. "Hemp Facts." Hemp Farm. http://hempfarm.org/Papers/Hemp_Facts.html.

Loos, Jessica. "Freedom Fighter of the Month: Alan Gordon: UV-B, Pot, the Law, and You." High Times No. 271. March 1998: letters.

Melanie Marquis *is a lifelong practitioner of magick. She is the author of* The Witch's Bag of Tricks *and the founder of United Witches global coven. A regular writer for the American Tarot Association and for Llewellyn's popular annuals, her work has appeared in many publications including* Pentacle Magazine, Witches and Pagans, *and* Circle. *A full-time mother, witch, and environmentalist, she's passionate about finding the mystical in the mundane through personalized magick and practical spirituality. www.melaniemarquis.com, www.unitedwitches.org, www.facebook.com/melaniemarquisauthor.*

Illustrator: Kathleen Edwards

Syncretism Versus Eclecticism

Gede Parma

I describe my personal path as syncretic rather than eclectic. I do so because I meaningfully, and with purpose, weave the diverse strands that inspire me into an aligned and conscious whole that is an expression of my unique self as a voyager through life. By identifying myself as syncretic, I believe I effectively communicate the dynamic of my personal spiritual path as holistic and impassioned with integrity and will. This is consistent with the Oxford Dictionary definition of *syncretism*, which speaks of the syncretic philosophy and practice as "the amalgamation or attempted amalgamation of different religions, cultures, or schools of thought." The ultimate goal is fusion—a union of a multitude of sources and schools of thought that relate to the individual, group, or culture. This is opposed to eclecticism, which Oxford defines as a philosophy that selects "doctrines from various schools of thought," with no aim of integration.

> **The ultimate goal is fusion—a union of a multitude of sources and schools of thought that relate to the individual, group, or culture.**

In past Pagan civilizations, we can regard the Hellenic/Greek world as extremely syncretic. The example that bears the most relevance to our world and culture today would be the Ptolemaic-founded city of Alexandria on the banks of the Nile delta. Alexandria was not only one of the busiest and most successful trading centers in the Alexandrian-Greek and later Roman world, it was also a melting pot of cultures and customs. The Kemetic (Egyptian) traditions of the people of the two lands gradually melded with the Greek and Homeric civic-approved ceremony, theology, and cosmology to create interesting additives to the overall tradition. One example of this is the striking figure of Serapis (Osiris in his fullness) who was identified with Amun, Zeus, Apis (the bull deity of Memphis), and Hades and was worshipped as the rising and dying vital force of the Nile.* Effectively speaking, a new deity was born that both

---

* Serapis was a king-force who held within himself the glorious lineage of Hades, King of the Underworld and collector of souls, and the multiple and diverse strengths and aspects of the native rising-dying deities. This was a God who had existed in many times and places prior to his birth in Alexandrian Egypt, but who became something apart from and autonomous within himself.

politically and culturally united the Egyptians and the Greeks. Serapis represented to Ptolemaic Egypt the overt anthropomorphism of the Hellenes fused with the grand lineage of localized spirits and cults that sustained the spiritual life of desert communities connected only by trade, whispered political rumors, and new gods. Many would consider the theology of identifying foreign deities with one's own pantheon in archetypal/sovereign-role resonance, as was the trend of the Roman emperors, a severely eclectic attribute; however, the compartmentalization of deities as relegated by role and aspect is a personal attitude that is not confined to either syncretics or eclectics. I personally know many eclectics who consider each deity a discrete and autonomous being within the Great Web.

I must make it clear that I do not regard self-professed eclectics as lesser or misinformed than myself. Unfortunately, over the past twenty or so years, the term *eclectic* as a spiritual indicator in the NeoPagan world has been tarnished by the misconception that eclectics are rampant "mish-mashers." For example, the common stereotype of an eclectic is an individual who misappropriates cultural customs and traditions and expresses that "whatever works" is the only factor for inclusion. Therefore, an eclectic may cast a Wiccan Circle, smudge with desert sage, and call upon Kali, while offering Kali bananas without concern for congruence or context, respect for cultural origins, or consideration of the efficacy of such things. While this is largely a stereotype, it is a gradual trend within NeoPaganism to casually adopt such an attitude.

All syncretists, by virtue of our nature, generally derive experience and inspiration from an eclectic framework.

Scott Cunningham first published *Wicca: A Guide for the Solitary Practitioner* in 1988 through Llewellyn Publications. Though *Wicca* was not the first book of its kind to offer an unbound and eclectic Wiccan framework, it was and is the most popular and has sold over 600,000 copies worldwide. I believe the ethics of integrity and the attitude of revolution underlined by respect found in Cunningham's books are the true essence and purpose of eclecticism: a spirit unbound by conservative dogma and doctrine, allowing for the inclusion and celebration of personal insight and gnosis, while actively seeking out the eternal wisdom of the worlds. This is definitely my framework, and as an avowed syncretist, I make the following point: *All syncretists, by virtue of our nature, generally derive experience and inspiration from an eclectic framework.*

Without having first been exposed to a world of infinite possibility and plurality, we are left void of any or all external forms or forces that may inspire, move, and challenge us. We begin a journey by first looking around the place in which we stand (the formative state of mind); we cast the Circle by taking in the horizon at all four directions and gesturing to the Above and then to the Below. Only at the culmination of this do we come to the center within—the womb of gestation, fermentation, and creation. The shadow-pooled refuge beneath the mighty Tree (which is the center within all things, including each of us) that popular Pagan author Christopher Penczak refers to as the place of rotting. This is the process by which we collect all that is of, by, and through us and allow it to mold, rot, and form organic compost. From this compost, potent seeds will grow into powerful trees, reflecting back to us the unique expression of spirit that is "I." It is here that the eclectic path becomes syncretic holism.

Those who know me personally and who have waxed eloquent with me on all manner of things relating to spirituality and magick would tend to regard me as a bit traditional, but also as a visionary who seeks wholeness and fullness in all things. My personal weekly ritual devotion is a testament and perfect expression of my spirituality and its nature.

During my devotional, I will perform a reconstructed and re-envisioned Greek cleansing of space rite; align with my ancestors and my spirits/deities of blood; honor Hekate as sovereign queen of witches and the Three Worlds; call in the Fey, spirits of place, the Tuatha, and the Shining Ones; cast a Circle thrice about in the name of Hekate and acknowledge and call in the elemental powers and guardians; and honor and align with my spirits/deities of breath/spirit.* I will then speak a prayer and carry on with the making

---

* My Gods of Breath/Spirit are those beings which I relate to on levels which aren't immediately apparent and are not directly related to my genetic ancestry. I tend to experience my Gods of Breath as karmic (e.g. past lives and devotions, etc.).

and blessing of offerings, the casting of spells, vision-journeying, trance work, etc. This ritual form has retained a basic skeleton for nearly six years, but has always been open to adaptation as I grow and evolve, forge new allyships* with the spirits and receive new insights and inspirations. There are elements of Hellenic ritual; Stregheria, Faerie, and Celtic ways; WildWood witchcraft; Balinese magick; and British Traditional Wicca in my devotion and thus in my path as a living thing. What makes these different traditions and cultures a part of the wholeness that is me is the consciousness I apply in creating a pathway that both grounds and refreshes me. I create in response to spiritual stimulus (either internal or external,

---

*This is the word I use to signify the spiritual significance of the connections and relationships we forge with the beings in the living world of which we are wholly a part.

if there is a difference) and so walk a path that is not the product of a mechanistic worldview, but of a magickal and mythical appreciation for the synchronicity and interconnection in life.

Syncretism demands that we uphold the ethics of integrity, that we abide by the laws of congruence rather than conformity, and that we honor and revel in the infinite realms of possibility as our primal foundation rather than as a transcendent ideal. A true eclectic, as Christopher Penczak postulates in his Living Temple books (Llewellyn), should aspire to know and experience all the manifold sources and streams that inspire and stimulate the mind, heart, soul, and body. As always, there is a fine line between spiritual syncretism and eclecticism. Journey well and blessed be.

Gede Parma *is a Witch, initiated Priest, and award-winning author. He is an initiate and teacher of the WildWood Tradition of witchcraft, a hereditary healer and seer with Balinese-Celtic ancestry, and an enthusiastic writer. Gede is a keen student of natural health therapies with a deep interest in herbal healing and nutrition. He is currently pursuing a bachelor of health science degree in these fields. He is the proud partner of a beautiful Virgo man and the devoted priest of the goddesses Persephone, Aphrodite, and Hekate. His spiritual path is highly syncretic and incorporates elements of traditional shamanism, Balinese Hinduism, British-Celtic witchcraft, Stregheria, Greek Paganism, Feri, Reclaiming, and WildWood witchcraft. You can visit Gede at www.gedeparma.com.*

Illustrator: Christa Marquez

But, You Don't Look Like a Witch

Mickie Mueller

I made my way through the city streets of St. Louis on my way to drop off a proof sheet and a disk of art files to one of our printers. You know, boring industry stuff for my day job. I could have passed for anyone in the pre-press business, wearing slacks, a conservative top with cardigan (perish the thought), and jewelry you can buy at any department store. No witchy boots on my feet nor pointy hat atop my auburn locks. So what's a nice witch like me doing in a getup like that? I had to ask myself, am I any less of a witch in my casual work attire, without even a small pentacle tucked inside my blouse?

Ok, all of us know that real witches don't have green skin, warts and wear pointy hats, right? Well, that old Halloween witch stereotype used to be what everyone in the mainstream world believed witches looked like. So are there new stereotypes of what witches should look like? And if so, where do these stereotypes come from, and are you "witchy enough" for your fellow witches? Do you lose your power without your pentagram on?

There are some in the Pagan community who seem very concerned about who looks witchy enough, or the importance of wearing your magical jewelry to every occasion, magical or mundane. Some people wear "witchy" garb everywhere they go, and kudos to those who can and do. There are also those in the community who—because of regional, work, family, or other reasons—are in no position to realistically go about in a swoosh of black with a big pentagram. For example, I would love to have a real estate agent who is also a witch, but I probably wouldn't want her wearing a flowing black cape and a pentagram the size of a hubcap while showing my home to a potential buyer. Why? I live in the real world, where a buyer might not be sympathetic to my personal religious choices. Those prejudices could make it hard for me to get my house sold, which could hurt my family and well-being. As a witch, my real estate agent might have plenty of magic tricks up her sleeve to help sell my house, and she doesn't need her best gothic gear to do it either.

I know a witch who works at a funky clothing boutique, and she dresses up everyday for work, and it's never a problem. But for her sister's baby shower, she toned it down. She wore nice casual clothing and left the witch-specific jewelry at home, because the gathering was about her sister and the exciting upcoming event, and she didn't want to take away from that. Another witch works for the public defender's office. She wears a suit to work and looks very professional, doesn't even wear a small pentagram hidden in her shirt (for her client's sake, she would never take a chance on it popping out in court). At a Pagan event, she's got her ritual garb on, and I've stood with her in a circle—she is a force to be reckoned with. I would dare anyone to say she's not witchy enough in her work clothes, jogging suit, or jeans. My point is that these two witches are who they are on the inside, with or without their witchy outfits.

The other side of the "not witchy enough" coin is the big Pagan festival where many people like to dress over the top, which, let's face it, is way fun. I love to wear my so-called "witchy" clothes to events where I'm meeting with other witches and Pagans. Flowing black, a sexy corset, a pirate shirt, or funky boots are a blast to wear, and it does make us feel witchy, doesn't it? I've also been to Pagan events where many people were totally casual—jeans, T-shirts, or even business casual. Some people might have their Born Again Pagan T-shirt on, and most wore their spiritual jewelry. I've actually seen some people at these events either snub one person for not dressing witchy enough, and another for being too theatrical and over the top. To me this is really unbelievable. As Pagans and witches, we need to stick together and not judge each other, especially for something as material and subjective as fashion. A Pagan festival should be a place to get away from worries about being judged. We get enough of that in the everyday world, we shouldn't have to worry about it from our fellow witches.

Allow me to illustrate this point. Below are descriptions of a few witches I know personally and what they are often seen wearing in the everyday world. You probably know at least some people who fit these descriptions. Don't think for a minute that any of these is more of a witch than the other; I've known powerful witches who have worked all of these styles and everything in between. One witch can change their look depending on where they plan to go, but the witch inside is what counts.

CORPORATE WITCH

This is the witch in the business world. This witch often wears a suit or slacks and blazer with a nice shirt because they understand that in the corporate world, such clothing is acceptable and portrays an illusion of power. Even to another witch, they might not be recognized, except for that certain air about them. Charisma, perhaps? This witch might have a small piece of magical jewelry tucked away somewhere, or maybe not. They also might have a piece much more subtle that they have enchanted the heck out of. This witch,

although totally incognito at work, probably has a closet full of the finest ritual wear you've ever seen.

BUSINESS CASUAL WITCH

The casual witch often comes in under the radar and can be seen in a blouse and slacks or really nice jeans for a woman, perhaps an oxford, designer T-shirt, or polo shirt for a man. This might be a teacher, PTA member, bartender, retailer, or someone you meet at a family gathering. This witch chooses the colors of their clothes for magical purposes for that day. They might wear New Age–style jewelry, such as magical stones/crystals or Celtic knots, in lieu of a pentagram or other witch-specific jewelry. Possibly wearing magical oils, this witch is keeping the world moving, working witchy ways behind the scenes with a quiet strength.

DAY-OFF WITCH

You've run into this witch at the store, on their day off, picking up milk, bread, and eggs or gassing up the car. Jeans or shorts, paired with who knows what, but sometimes it'll be a sci-fi/fantasy T-shirt, or even a T-shirt proclaiming their witch status. After all, it's their day off! You're likely to spot the tell tale pentagram, Greenman, or Goddess jewelry, though it may be tucked depending how far out of the broom closet they are.

HIPPIE WITCH

Broom stick skirts, tie-dye, batik, and funky embroidered clothes made in India are the mainstay for this free spirit. You can see the hippie witch sporting their style working at a record store, boutique, on their days off, or at a Pagan Festival. The hippie witch is often in a setting where witch-specific jewelry is not a big deal at all, so they're probably wearing plenty of it mixed with hippie stuff. Magical oils are a great scent for this witch, either pure or blended.

Gothy/Classic Witch

Black, red, and purple are some of the shades you'll see the goth or classic witch wearing. Anything with an old world flair, medieval lace-up stuff, like you might find in Bram Stoker's closet. This witch probably owns some fabulous pointy witch hats. Classic witchy boots, combat boots, or anything in between will be seen stomping

out this high fashion witchy style. Any witch-specific jewelry will be worn right out in the open. Dramatic makeup finishes this wild witchy look. You'll probably spot this witch out for the night or at indoor events (some outdoor events are too hot for this style).

. . . .

So which witch is the witchiest? All of them! These can be, and often are, the same witch on different days. The important thing to remember is that whether you look like an obvious witch to anyone on the street or not, a witch is who you are on the inside. It's a belief, a faith, a way of life, and it doesn't matter what you look like. You can take away all the trappings of a witch, but the person inside is still the same. You are a magical person whether you're in a business suit, jogging suit, or ritual robes, and if you believe in your magic, you have nothing to prove!

So, it turns out that my business slacks and cardigan are actually my witchy clothes. Do you know why? Because it's a real witch wearing them.

Mickie Mueller is an award-winning and critically acclaimed artist of fantasy, fairy, and myth. She is an ordained Pagan minister and has studied natural magic, Celtic tradition, and Faerie Tradition. She is also a Reiki healing master/teacher in the Usui Shiki Royoho Tradition. She enjoys creating magical art full of fairies, goddesses, and beings of folklore. She works primarily in a mix of colored pencil and watercolor infused with magical herbs corresponding to her subject matter. Mickie is the illustrator of The Well Worn Path and The Hidden Path tarot decks and the writer/illustrator of The Voice of the Trees, A Celtic Ogham Divination Oracle from Llewellyn. Mickie is a regular article contributor to several of Llewellyn's annuals.

Illustrator: Tim Foley

Witch Parent

Dallas Jennifer Cobb

This article is about being Wiccan or Pagan and a parent. It's not a "how-to" article, but a personal discussion of the joys and pains of parenting in a mainstream society, maintaining my faith in isolation and changing times, and coming into a different sort of magical community through my child. It is also about what this process has taught me about being Pagan.

Sometimes it feels like there's a constant choice to be made between "belonging" and being Pagan. With a child in the public school system, Pagan parents often face the challenge of deciding "which" parent to be at any given time: the Pagan parent or the mainstream parent.

But over time, both parenting and mainstream society have taught me profound lessons about being a better Pagan. I have come to see that I can be both a practicing Pagan and a good parent, all at the same time. No longer wondering "which" parent to be, I know I am a "Witch" parent.

Nothing Remains the Same

For many of us, faith is a very personal matter, as is our Pagan practice. We develop our own interpretation of what it means to be Pagan. We seek out like-minded people and take part in circles, rituals, and community gatherings that reflect our understanding of the craft.

Because being Pagan has historically meant being an "outsider," we are comfortable with being unique and making individual choices about our beliefs, identity, and magical practices. And our magical communities are usually comprised of people who share similar ideas, ideals, and practices.

But once we have children, who we are and how we are changes. This catalyst causes change to ripple throughout our entire lives, changing our Pagan practice and our magical communities.

For many new parents, the change in their Pagan practice and community coincides with the birth of their baby. Perhaps the Moon circles meet too late at night for the baby, imbibing at rituals feels alien for the nursing mom, or the sky-clad Sabbat celebrants don't seem like an ideal mix with young children. After the birth of a child, many aspects of the Pagan practice and community that were previously unquestioned and accepted can feel unsettling, unwanted, or even unsafe.

Winds of Change

When I had my daughter, I felt very protective. I no longer felt safe at the wild and rollicking Pagan gatherings I used to enjoy so much. I found the imbibing of alcohol (and sometimes drugs) worrisome. I was leery of the blatantly sexual energy that wafted around at rituals. And because I couldn't change these things—indeed had always previously enjoyed them—I realized that I needed to change.

Drawn to the quiet safety of home and hearth that felt cozy and protective, not just for me but for my baby, my Pagan practice shifted from very communal and community-driven to a solitary, private practice.

Drawn to the quiet safety of home that felt cozy and protective … my Pagan practice shifted from very communal and community-driven to a solitary, private practice.

My Moon circle disappeared first. Comprised of child-free adults, they wanted to continue to meet at night, often very late at night, and that didn't work for me as the parent of an infant. While struggling to decide what to do, how to balance my Pagan circle and my parenting, I was told very plainly that children were not welcome in the circle. That made the choice an easy one: I left the circle.

Community rituals and Sabbat celebrations disappeared next. Because my circle and therefore my community were mostly child-free adults, I didn't feel comfortable taking my baby to rituals. Everyone seemed to expect her to be absolutely silent. She wasn't a cry-baby, but a cooer. Still, her sounds of pleasure and wonder drew looks of scorn and whispers, which drained my energy. And so I stopped attending community rituals and celebrations.

My summer sojourns to witch camp also ceased. Sure, there was a camp that welcomed children, but when I contemplated packing up all the stuff needed for baby and me, along with the reality of camping out with her for a week, I was exhausted just thinking about it. So, I didn't go.

With a baby only a few months old, I found myself totally alone in my Pagan practice.

A New Path

As a new mother, I became a solitary practitioner, with my home, hearth, and family at the center of my Pagan practice. I created rituals, magical craft, and Sabbat celebrations for my little family. My home became a magical realm, steeped in altars and sacred spaces. I conducted Moon rituals for just myself and my infant daughter. Swaddled in the warmth of my arms, I took her out to meet the Moon. And the Goddess welcomed her, asleep or awake, cooing or crying.

In those early years, with a sleeping or breast-feeding babe in my arms, and later with an active toddler, I worked a lot of solitary magic, casting spells, manifesting, chanting, and celebrating in the comfort and safety of my home. And as she grew, my daughter came to love the craft, learning seasonal stories, making magical crafts, and participating in rituals.

All was well on my new path until my daughter went off to school. The wheel of time turned again and our little world expanded beyond the confines of home and hearth, family, and friends as a result of my daughter's new community.

Finding Magic Everywhere

"Magic is the movement of natural energies to create needed change," writes Scott Cunningham in *Spell Crafts* (Llewellyn, 1993). And when I let go of my narrow scope of what a magical community ought to look like, I started to see magic everywhere.

On the first day of school, I walked my daughter up to the school, sent her into the play yard, and stood outside the gate with the parents of the other kids in her class. I heard many spells of protection cast, blessings, and repeated reminders of the Wiccan Rede.

Parents were telling their children "Listen to your teacher, and they will help you" (Bide the Wiccan Law ye must, in perfect love

and perfect trust), "Have fun, and no one gets hurt" (An ye harm none, do as ye will), "Be good and good things will happen" (What ye send out, comes back to thee), and "I will be waiting right here for you after school. I love you" (Merry meet and merry part, and merry meet again).

So I widened my concept of Pagan practice. Instead of limiting it to the stereotypes I held, I allowed for the possibility that the same concepts were at the root of almost every spiritual and religious practice. Essentially, everyone was striving to live their lives by the same principles I was.

I allowed for the possibility that the same concepts were at the root of almost every spiritual and religious practice. Essentially, everyone was striving to live their lives by the same principles I was.

Starhawk says that "each individual is a living embodiment of the sacred. The divine experience is equally available to all, and each person's experience of the divine is valid and important."* When I watched parents with their children, I was able to see first the child, and later the parent, as a living embodiment of the sacred. And it helped me to see that love was at the root of that sacred practice.

A New Circle

The other moms (and a few dads) who dropped off and picked up children in front of the school were easy acquaintances with whom

---

*Starhawk. "A Working Definition of Reclaiming." Reweaving. http://www.reweaving.org/tradition.html.

I shared these daily magical rituals. They were a cluster of people who usually stood in a small circle, exchanging news, gossip, and advice. Soon, I learned that they also knew a lot about "magic."

From them I learned the magical formulas for getting rid of head lice, the manifestation spell and incantation to use with teachers to manifest extra support in class, and tried-and-true spells for stopping bullies. Even though these were not Pagan moms, I had to concede that in their circle, they were working big magic.

I was also invited to participate in "rituals." The Samhain ritual of sugar feasting held school-wide, the annual Yule celebration concert, and the Ostara weekend festival of magical crafts, feasting, and egg hunts.

With school counsel, I did big group prosperity "magic." Starting with a dilapidated playground, we manifested money, supplies, and workers, and created a magical playground. An enchantment spell was cast on the principal who intoned the power of the project. We conjured a binding spell on the school board, and they used "found" magic to manifest a hidden source of money to build the new playground.

And here I thought I was the only one who believed in magic!

Within the school, I got involved with classroom tutoring and found a place to work my own brand of magic. I taught kids affirmations that enabled them to believe in their powers. I facilitated rituals and rites that led to the memorization of alphabets, numbers, and rhymes. I taught the magical art of decoding letters and words, and I led recreational clubs that incorporated meditation, reflection, and focused intention.

When I really opened my eyes, I saw magic being practiced all around me.

Living In Translation

Learning how to express my faith to my new acquaintances has required some spellwork of my own. I have had to use incantation carefully. Living in a small rural community, I have had to find ways to communicate my faith to people that don't alienate me or my family or frighten the parents of my daughter's playmates.

I found that all I need to do is tell the truth, but to do so in terms that other people might more readily understand and accept. Instead of saying "I'm a Pagan and worship the Goddess at her Sabbats and full moons," I can easily state my beliefs in language more familiar and acceptable to mainstream people. I rely on the metaphors of gardening, agriculture, and nature to express my magical thoughts and beliefs, and often refer to the moon as a point of reference, one that is readily understood by the farmers and herds' people in the community.

I have also relied heavily on old adages that are common to our region and community, adages that clearly express some of the tenets of my Pagan faith. Using these adages, I have found a commonality of belief and faith: "What goes around comes around" I say, or "That is going to come back on him, three fold," and "Cheaters never prosper."

I have learned over time that speaking in adages, metaphors, and parables is a powerful magical tool, enabling me to connect with many people of varied and different faiths. Because I have translated my purely Pagan patter into something more universal and symbolic in nature, I have found points of commonality and agreement. And by using adages, metaphors, and symbols, I can talk in detail about my Pagan faith and still be understood conceptually by Christians and others in my community.

Finding Community

Since my daughter started school, I have moved from a solitary practitioner to one who celebrates very loudly and publicly within a large community.

I have taken part in rituals, feasts, and Sabbat celebrations, and I have worked "magic" both alone and in community. I have seen how everyday people can move natural energy to create needed change, and the result is magical indeed.

While many of the people who are part of our school community don't identify themselves as Pagans, with them I have found a safe place to celebrate, affirm, worship, and praise the Goddess as she manifests herself in her purest form: through our children.

RESOURCES FOR PAGAN PARENTS

Carson, Anne, ed. *Caretaking a New Soul—Writings on Parenting from Thich Nhat Hanh to Z. Budapest.* Freedom, CA: The Crossing Press, 1999

McCleary, Patrick. "PaganDad." http://www.Pagandad.com/.
  I love that McCleart's subtext is "Leading the Next Generation Forward Through Faith." I think that says it all.

Starhawk, Diane Baker, and Anne Hill. *Circle Round: Raising children in Goddess Traditions.* New York: Bantam Books, 1998.

Wigington, Patti. "Your Rights as a Pagan Parent." About.com http://Paganwiccan.about.com/od/yourlegalrights/a/Rights_Parents.htm.

WitchVox. "Pagan Parenting." http://www.witchvox.com/_x.html?c=parent.
  This page is filled with tons of articles, resources, opinions, and links that will make you feel rich and connected.

Life is what you make it, and **Dallas Jennifer Cobb** *has made a magical life in a waterfront village on the shores of great Lake Ontario. Forever scheming novel ways to pay the bills, she practices manifestation magic and wildlands witchcraft. She currently teaches Pilates, works in a library, and writes to finance long hours spent following her hearts' desire—time with family, in nature and on the water. Contact her at jennifer.cobb@live.com.*

Illustrator: Rik Olson

Reconsidering the Spectre of Pagan Standard Time

Susan Pesznecker, On-Time Pagan

Imagine this: You spend hours, no, days planning the perfect ritual for your coven, including an agreed-upon start time of 8:00 pm that coincides with everyone's home, kid, pet, gym, and work schedules. BlackBerries and iPhones are synched. As the lead organizer, you've poured heart and soul into the preparations, and at 7:45, you're garbed and ready, haunting the front door and excited for the evening to begin. Problem is, no one else has arrived. Eight o'clock comes and goes … 8:10 … 8:25 … Finally, at 8:30, someone shows up and then others begin to

48

trickle in. By the time all the key players have shown up, it's 9:15. The ritual that should have been over by now—leaving plenty of time for fellowship and a table of cakes and ale—hasn't even started. You want to go ahead and start, but others insist on waiting for the remaining stragglers. In the meantime, one couple looks anxiously at the time and announces they only have a babysitter for another forty-five minutes.

You're madder than h…. Well, you know. And you're a victim of Pagan Standard Time.

What is Pagan Standard Time? Somehow, somewhere along the line, an unfortunate urban myth took root within the Pagan community. Referred to as Pagan Standard Time or PST, it goes something like this: If you're an hour late for a ritual, circle, class, or other event, you're on time. If you're two hours late, you're still on time. If you don't show up at all, that's okay too.

Huh?

No one seems sure how or when this mythos got started, but it appears to coincide with the development of the Neo-Pagan movement. But why? Why are Pagans (and presumably Wiccans, Druids, Chaos Mages, Faeries, etc.) willing to treat members of their communities so shabbily?

It may date back to the modern beginnings of Neo-Paganism, at least here in the United States. The most visible parts of religious America consist of mainstream religions; many of these are fundamentalist and most look askance at those following Earth-based traditions, criticizing them for not following the mainstream status quo. Pagans, in response, may have rebelled with, "Oh, yeah? We'll just show you exactly how non-mainstream we can be!" This could easily have led to the hippie-style, self-doctrinal approach of ignoring schedules, clocks, and agendas and refusing to comply with any sort of structured obligation.

Speaking of structure: some Pagans feel that timepieces and any sort of framework or schedule have the potential to interfere with the natural flow of energy raising, ritual, etc. These folks eschew timepieces, preferring a loose, organic process and allowing each stage to happen as it will, following the universe's flow and rhythm. Alas, as busy as people are today, there often isn't time for this kind of natural unfolding, which is exactly why rituals and events are usually scheduled for a specific time and in a set place.

Alas, as busy as people are today, there often isn't time for this kind of natural unfolding, which is exactly why rituals and events are usually scheduled for a specific time and in a set place.

A practical line of reasoning supporting PST might have to do with energy disruption of watches and electronics. Simply said, when magick is in the air, electronics and digital items often fail for inexplicable reasons. So, some ask, why court disaster by wearing them? The result is predictable: if no one knows what time it is, it's pretty hard to stay on schedule.

The online Urban Dictionary defines Pagan Standard Time as either "fashionably late, when preceded by a definite hour," or "within half an hour or so of" a specified time. The Llewellyn Online Encyclopedia describes PST as "a joking reference to the common experience of Pagan rituals starting later than planned or announced due to not having preparations completed or awaiting participants who are arriving late." The Arcane Crafts witches Annual takes the "joke" idea even further, suggesting a schematic for a clock that runs only on Pagan Standard Time. The prototype has no second hand because "no Pagan runs on

THAT tight a schedule." The clock features the traditional minute and hour hands but also has a third "Pagan hand" that runs at half the speed of the others. The clock face has thirteen hours instead of twelve—effectively adding two extra hours to each day—but the hours from five o'clock to eight o'clock are missing, assuming that Pagans simply aren't awake or functional during those parts of the day.

But here's the thing: although this is all tongue-in-cheek and elbow-poke-in-the-ribsey, PST really isn't that funny. Fritz Jung, co-founder of the well-known WitchVox website, says, "Many witches, Wiccans, and Pagans have a cute little phrase that they like to banter about called Pagan Standard Time. This means they show up to whatever, whenever they please and completely oblivious to the time that they have 'committed' to. Personally, I loathe this convenient little phrase." When a circle mate plans a gorgeous ritual and

you show up an hour late, it's not cool or casual or rebellious—it's just plain rude. When one of your grove members plays a key role in the local Pagan Pride celebration, only to find that most of the people who agreed to help disappeared in the last two weeks, leaving a scramble to fill in the holes they've left, their behavior is thoughtless. When a coven's year-and-a-day planners work for months to create a schedule and members repeatedly show up half an hour late for every class or unprepared to teach the sessions they agreed to lead … Well, you know.

Let's take this a few steps further and consider several reasons why competent, practical, and ethical magick users should give up the practice or acceptance of PST.

First, for those who follow the Wiccan Rede as a core ethic, reflect on "And it harm none, do what ye will." Showing up late or blowing off commitments arguably causes harm by leaving fellow group members feeling frustrated or disrespected. I think everyone would agree that good magick is not borne from a cauldron of annoyance.

Then there's the magickal Law of Cause and Effect, which concerns the nature of action and reaction. Strings of poorly planned or chaotic magickal workings tend to produce fragmented, choppy results. This isn't what most of us aspire to in our magickal workings. It also leaves one subject to the idea of magickal rebound: send something ill-conceived or uneven out into the Universe, and you're going to get the same thing (or worse) back. A group that does not begin, work, and end together also tweaks the Law of Sympathetic Magick, which addresses affinities and interactions between people, materials, and intentions.

Speaking of intention, the Law of Positive Attraction says that like attracts like. In a group setting, creating a desired reality requires a conscious, coordinated effort between like-intentioned folks. How can a ritual or magickal effort raise energy or muster focused intent when it must continually stop and start to admit late arrivals or when it lacks the strength of a full coterie of members? Ill-planned magick may also backfire through the Law of Association, which suggests that the more commonality acts of magick share, the greater their influence. If one has a full coven working to work magick or raise energy, the commonality of pattern and intention has a much stronger influence and result than does a working that is fractured or splintered by late arrivals or missing members.

Let's talk ethics as well, specifically, having respect for others and an awareness of basic ethical tenets—and of time. If you're invited to an event that others have planned, simple courtesy requires you to respect their efforts and comply. To be carelessly or intentionally late is akin to telling the planners that you don't care. As for practicing PST, it may threaten one's accountability, leaving people to believe the planner-without-a-schedule cannot keep a promise, fulfill an obligation, or be trusted. It's hard to create relationships this way, and repeat offenders may end up paying the ultimate price: those who are habitually late and don't seem to care may find they're no longer invited to events, festivals, rituals, or other celebrations.

In his WitchVox article, "Unchecked Pagan Standard Time (PST) Erodes Pagan Community Viability," Aldous Tyler points out a potential image problem associated with PST, namely the negative view that it may present to the public. Tyler remarks, "What begin

> **If one has a full coven working to work magic or raise energy, the commonality of pattern and intention has a much stronger influence and result.**

as habits turn into norms, which in turn become standards, and these can affect how the community is perceived both from within and without." The human is a highly adaptive creature, and when patterns of lateness recur, many communities adapt to the repetitive time shift—the PST—rather than resisting it. It's the Law of Negative Attraction in action. Over time, this can snowball to a state where there is little or no order, leading many to give up rather than participate. In today's setting, where Pagans work for recognition and credibility from the non-Pagan community and where public ritual is a great way to attract potential members, the disorganization spawned by PST isn't doing us any favors. Simply said, Pagans don't need the bad press.

Is PST always a bad thing? No, not always. We've all attended über-casual events where there was no schedule and everything happened when it happened. Sometimes there's joy in setting aside the clock and simply going with the flow. Good organizers are always "flegid": flexible + rigid. They know that it's sometimes important to color outside the lines, but they still keep an eye on the schedule to ensure that the event proceeds as it should.

Let's consider the organizer: the person who steps up and says "I'll be in charge," volunteering his or her time to make an event happen. This wonderful person has earned the right to make the decisions. If you volunteer to plan a major Sabbat event, for example, and you're a person who absolutely adores the loosey-gooseyness associated with PST, you have every right to avoid a rigid timetable— or any agenda at all, if that's your choice. But you're ethically obliged to let your participants know that the schedule is non-existent and/ or likely to change. Likewise, if you're a by-the-minute planner, you should do everything in your power to communicate that your event is scheduled and will begin on time whether everyone is present or not. Once you've made this known, be sure to start and stop on time! Develop a consistent reputation and people will take you seriously: they'll either show up on time or, if they find the schedule too constricting, they'll avoid your events. Either way, you're in the clear.

How can you protect yourself from PST fallout? If you're attending someone else's event, ask specific questions about when the action will really start and plan accordingly. Throw a camp chair, a thermos of coffee or tea, and a good book into your car and you'll be all set to wait out a late start. If you're attending a seminar, class, or other public event, do your best to follow the schedule. Remember that the teachers and presenters are usually donating their time and often their own money as well. They may have traveled a long way to get to the event and may be paying for hotel, food, babysitter, boarding the dog, etc. Honor their efforts by respecting their itineraries.

Practically speaking, with the technology available today, there's no reason to ever be late. By planning ahead, knowing the schedule, and using the capabilities of one's favorite smart phone, laptop calendar, wristwatch, or sundial, we'll arrive on time—or even early. By arriving on time, we show respect for the magick and our fellow magick users. Let's set aside the shabby practice of Pagan Standard Time—our magickal community will reap the benefits!

Resources, *Accessed August 2010*

Jung, Fritz. "What is a Witch War?" Witchvox.com. http://www.witchvox .com/va/dt_va.html?a=usfl&c=wars&id=2093.

Llewellyn Worldwide. "Pagan Standard Time." The Llewellyn Encyclopedia. http://www.llewellyn.com/encyclopedia/term/ Pagan+Standard+Time.

"Pagan Standard Time Clock." http://www.turoks.net/Cabana/Pagan StandardTime.htm.

Tyler, Aldous. "Unchecked Pagan Standard Time (PST) Erodes Pagan Community Viability." http://mabon-fest.grouply.com/message/309.

Susan "Moonwriter" Pesznecker *is a writer, college English teacher, nurse, and hearth Pagan living in northwestern Oregon. She holds a masters degree in nonfiction writing and loves to read, watch the stars, camp with her wonder-poodle, and work in her own biodynamic garden. Sue is Dean of Students and teaches nature studies and herbology in the online Grey School of Wizardry (greyschool.com). She's the author of* Gargoyles *(New Page, 2007) and* Crafting Magick with Pen and Ink *(Llewellyn, 2009) and is a regular contributor to many of the Llewellyn annuals. Visit Sue on her Facebook page at http://www.facebook.com/ susan.pesznecker.*

Illustrator: Bri Hermanson

Should You Do Magic for a Cause or Donate Money?

Lupa

When popular Pagan author Isaac Bonewits was dying from cancer in 2010, members of the community around the world participated in two separate rituals to help him. The first, the Rolling Thunder ritual, was created by Isaac's wife Phaedra as a way to build up a cascade of healing energy for him. People were asked to perform their healing rituals at 9 pm in their respective time zones in order to create a continuous flow of magic for the stated intent.

The second ritual was the Rolling Coin ritual. On the full moon in July,

Pagans were asked to donate what they could to help the Bonewits family cover expenses for medical and other bills. Isaac's family had quite a bit of debt, not surprising given that even those cancer patients with insurance can still be expected to pay staggering copays, nevermind the costs not covered by any insurance.

I don't have, nor do I believe anyone has, accurate numbers as to how many people participated in each ritual. However, anecdotally speaking, most of the comments on the Rolling Thunder ritual were of the "I did it!" variety, while many of the comments regarding the Rolling Coin ritual said "I wish I could, but…"

While this was a pretty high-profile example, I've seen this pattern occur countless times over the years I've been a part of the Pagan community. People are very quick to light a candle or say a prayer, but ask them to open their wallets, even for a few dollars,

and suddenly there's a murmuring of "Can't, sorry." And anyone who's ever put together a Pagan event knows how hard it is to get people to dedicate even an hour of their time in volunteer work.

This leads me to wonder whether "sending energy" is a cop-out to make people feel better about not giving more tangible, record-able help. When you encounter a need, is it better to do magic for the cause or donate monetary help?

What Do (Or Don't) We Have to Offer?

Don't get me wrong. I'm well aware of the economic situation in the world right now. And it's common knowledge that neopagan-ism is not a demographic with a particularly high median income (though there are more white collar and other well-paid workers in our ranks than some may assume), but we're not all starving artists and baristas. And not everyone has the time to do things like event organization, between work, family, and so forth. So these criticisms don't apply across the board.*

It also seems as though there are a lot of hands stretched out for money these days. Whether it's Pagan businesses struggling to stay open or individuals losing their jobs and needing help covering mortgages and other bills, a lot of folks are in dire straits.

Perhaps that's why so many perceive themselves as unable to do-nate money to any cause. Often it feels like we're having to count our dollars just to make sure there's enough left to still be eating at the end of the pay period. So we may not like letting even a few of those dollars slip away to something where we aren't getting any-thing in return. (Why else do you think so many nonprofit groups

---

* Plus I realize that most people who see any resemblance to themselves in this article may be leaping to their own defense, perhaps even without thinking about it.

sell T-shirts, stuffed animals, and other tangibles to make money, despite also taking donations?)

Volunteering takes, obviously, time. And if you're working a couple of jobs to make ends meet, or if you work and have children, or otherwise are really busy, it may feel like there's simply no time to offer people you may not know very well, for little to no personal return beyond "a job well done." And especially if you see your festivals and other Pagan events as vacation time, the last thing you may want to do is work, even if it's volunteer work. It's certainly easy to come up with excuses not to give away your time or your money.

Does Magic Actually Work for this Stuff?

To be quite honest, I have trouble seeing magic as an equal effort as compared to donations and volunteering. While I have been practicing magic for well over a decade, I see it as a much more fickle and less objectively dependable thing than more mundane efforts. I generally feel it's better suited for particularly subjective and personal causes than something like "save the world!"

Are you familiar with confirmation bias? A very simple and incomplete definition would be "seeing what one wants to see." In the case of magic, most people who practice it want to believe that it works (especially on an objective level), and so, whether consciously or not, will emphasize results that favor that interpretation.

For example, let's say you do ten spells. Of those ten spells, three of them are followed by getting what you wanted, three with something sort of like what you wanted but not exactly, and four with not getting what you wanted. A 30 percent success rate isn't all that great. However, confirmation bias may lead you to count the three kinda-sorta "results" as successes because they were in the neighborhood of what you wanted. And then you can come up with any

number of justifications involving outside factors that led to the other four simply not working at all.

With magic that doesn't work, you can't reliably trace whether it had an effect or not. In fact, you can't even trace it necessarily when it does work. There's no way to prove that the spell or ritual you performed actually had any effect compared to if you hadn't done the magic.

With donations and volunteering, on the other hand, it's easy to see where the effort goes and what the result is. The exact dollars you give may be tough to trace, but you can definitely see where your volunteer time goes. I spent some time volunteering with Habitat for Humanity, and at the end of the day I could say "I nailed some hurricane strips to the roof" or "I painted a couple hundred feet of siding."

So, at least as far as being able to claim definite, measurable results, donations and volunteering has the upper hand.

Magic As a Way to Assuage Guilt

Most people want to be able to help others in some way. There's absolutely nothing wrong with this. However, I think sometimes "sending energy" is used as a way to make a person feel better about not being able to give money or time. And, beyond that, I think "sending energy" is sometimes used as an excuse to not give time or money, even when those things are available.

If you see the intangible effort of magic as equal to the tangible efforts of donations and volunteering, then it's easy to make the excuse of "Well, I'll just light a candle/say a prayer/do a spell." Rarely do people spend as much time and money on a magical working as they would on a donation or volunteering effort. I generally don't spend twenty-five dollars or more on candles and other supplies for a single magical act, and while I'll happily spend seven hours on a Habitat build, I think my personal record for an ongoing ritual is something under two hours.

Let's face it—for the most part, doing magic just doesn't require as many resources as more mundane activities. And I think because of that a lot of people use magic as their excuse for not putting in the time or money in other ways. I'm not talking about people who are completely strapped for cash or spare time, but the ones who could give up buying a new tarot deck or watching a bad movie, even just once, to put those efforts toward something other than themselves.

> Rarely do people spend as much time and money on a magical working as they would on a donation or volunteering effort.

We do deserve nice things, but sometimes giving up an unneces-
sary bauble can make the crucial difference to someone who's just
trying to get by.

Appraising Intent

So, be honest with yourself. Whenever you're faced with someone
asking for your time or money and you opt to work magic instead,
look at why you made that decision. Is it because giving even five
dollars or less would seriously affect your finances? (Yes, this is possible.) Is it because you just don't have the time or sanity to make
one more commitment? (This is entirely possible, too.)

Or are you making an excuse? Could you give just a couple of
bucks or a half an hour of time, but instead choose to stay at home
and light a candle? Are there places where you could give up some
small luxury to make the money or time for someone else, but instead write down an intent on a piece of paper to burn? If you find
you are making excuses, there's no need or gain in beating yourself
up about it. Just make different choices to the best of your ability,
and move on.

It Really Doesn't Take Much

The saying "every little bit counts" is true. To give you a personal
example, I am an artist and author. I sell my art and books at local
Pagan events. While I have a lot of big, expensive, shiny objects for
sale, like bone athames and elaborate totem dance costumes, I also
have smaller, inexpensive things like little leather pouches and ear-
rings. Sure, selling a couple of the big items can make my weekend
a lot happier. But I sell a lot more of the little things, because that's
what more folks can afford, and those add up pretty quickly.

When someone asking for donations says "Even a few dollars will help," they mean it. Maybe you can't offer fifty dollars, but three or four or five is more than nothing at all. If a whole bunch of people give that small amount, it does add up. But even if it's just you, it's that little bit more that the cause has to work with.

The same thing goes for volunteering. Maybe you can't spend hours organizing an event or cooking food at a festival. But maybe you can proofread some advertising copy, or post something promotional on your blog. Again, cumulative small efforts do add up, and putting forth a little effort does more than putting forth none at all.

And, if after giving time and/or money you decide to work magic to "help things along," there's nothing wrong with that, either.

RESOURCES, *Accessed August 2010*

Clark, Jennifer. "A Call to Create a Rolling Thunder for Isaac Bonewits." Examiner.com. http://www.examiner.com/paganism-in-national/a-call-to-create-a-rolling-thunder-for-isaac-bonewits.

The Wild Hunt. "Pagan Community Notes" July 24, 2010. http://wildhunt.org/blog/2010/07/pagan-community-notes-adf-fundraiser-isaac-bonewits-sj-tucker-and-more.html.

Lupa *is a neoshaman, Pagan author, and ritual tool artist living in Portland, Oregon. She may be found online at http://www.thegreenwolf.com and http://therioshamanism.com.*

Illustrator: Kathleen Edwards

Witchy Living

DAY-BY-DAY WITCHCRAFT

Ten-Minute Magickal Meals

Melanie Marquis

I love magick, but it's not always easy to find the quiet time required for complex spells and elaborate rituals. When I can't enjoy the luxury of a full-blown magick session, I look for other ways to enrich my practice and embrace the witchy lifestyle. Magickal cooking offers a way to do just that: practice spellcasting techniques, promote magickal growth, expand awareness, and support positive change, all without taking up a single extra minute in an already busy day.

Magickal cooking is the practice of directing personal energy and magickal power to produce desired results through the mechanics of food preparation, and it doesn't take any longer than regular cooking. With these easy and practical ideas, you'll be out of the kitchen in ten minutes flat, as an everyday chore becomes a pleasant opportunity to further experience the power that magickal practice brings to light.

With magickal cooking, we get the most out of every meal, and it's easy to master. All you need to get started is an understanding of three basic techniques—stirring, slicing, and heating—and a few handy hints and you'll be reaping the rewards of magickal cooking in no time, infusing your practice, your food, and your life with new power.

Magickal Mudra Mixing

Adapted from a yoga technique, Hasta Mudras, or hand postures, can add powerful energy to your food while you stir. Forming the Mudras balances *prana*, the life force, and aligns our body, mind, and spirit into a harmonic and empowered state. Magickal Mudra mixing awakens and balances our personal energy, bestowing these same benefits on the food being prepared. Ingredients take on the energetic imprint of the Mudra as you stir, making for a powerfully magickal meal that feeds the spiritual body as well as the physical.

The first step of Mudra Mixing is to choose a Mudra that corresponds to the vibration you wish to bring to the food. Try the Pran Mudra (touch tips of ring finger and pinky to tip of thumb) to increase the vital energy of your recipe ingredients. For stress relief and to impart a relaxing quality to your food, the Gyan Mudra (touch tip of thumb to tip of index finger) works well. For variety, check out a book on Hasta Mudras and don't be afraid to experiment—only through exploration will you discover the Mudras that work best for you.

Once you've chosen a Mudra, it's time to mix. As you stir with one hand, form the Mudra with your other hand and hold it several inches above the bowl or pot. As the energy, or prana, in your hands is brought into an ordered alignment, visualize this same effect taking place within the food as you mix. I like to carry the visualization further, imagining in my mind's eye exactly what I want to achieve. For example, when I mix ingredients while forming the Gyan Mudra, I visualize stress in my body and environment diminishing, spiraling off into the distance with each stir.

Spellcasting With a Knife

You can also add power to your magickal meals by slicing ingredients with an empowered blade, a knife charmed to cast your spell into the food with each cut. Hold the knife in your hand while focusing on what you want your magick to achieve. When the energy is at its height, cast it into the knife, sending it in through the handle to flow to the very tip of the blade. As you cut, feel the energies of the knife coursing through the food, charming it with your magickal intent.

You can also add numerology to the slicing process, cutting food into a certain number of slices best suited to your particular working. For example, if you're making a meal to enhance natural beauty, slice your ingredients into six pieces (or if large, cut in sets of six), the number associated with beauty and perfection. Here are a few key words to get you started:

1. Leadership, Courage, Creativity
2. Cooperation, Understanding, Forgiveness
3. Sociable, Charming, Friendly

4. Reliable, Determined, Loyal

5. Adventure, Intelligence, Humor

6. Persuasive, Peaceful, Angelic

7. Mystical, Thoughtful, Artistic

8. Power, Success, Wisdom

9. Excitement, Curiosity, Spirituality

Turn Up the Heat, Turn Up the Magick

You can add a touch of nature magick to the cooking process by charming your stove to mimic the power of the sun or the fire element. Simply call on these forces and invite them into your stove, asking that the appliance be charmed and blessed. If you like, place a candle or a symbol of the sun on the stovetop. As you heat food, be it on the top of the stove or in the oven, think of the magickal energies in the ingredients expanding. Visualize the activity of the molecules within the food as they become excited when heated, increasing their speed and motion and activating your magick.

You can add the magick in with a dash of spice or a wave of your wand right at the end. Or, you can make every step of the process magickally aligned with your goal …

Designing Ten-Minute Magickal Meals

A meal can be made magickal with one little touch or with magick infused in every step of the process. You can add the magick in with a dash of spice or a wave of your wand right at the end. Or, you can make every step of the process magickally aligned with your goal,

choosing every ingredient based on its attributes and preparing the food while fully focused on your intent and the working at hand. It's up to you and how much energy and attention you want to devote to your magick in the ten minutes of cooking time.

Not every ingredient needs to be in line with your spell goal, but if possible it's nice to have at least two ingredients that compliment each other magickally. You can choose spices based on traditional attributes found in an encyclopedia of herbs or vegetables based on color attributes, associated symbolism, or folklore; use your imagination and trust your magick!

Now of course, getting in and out of the kitchen and working magick while you're at it in just ten minutes flat is no easy task. Many foods require a longer cooking time and aren't going to work when you're in a rush. But there are a few staples that can be widely adapted to a variety of recipes and that cook very quickly. Pastas, wraps, and chilies are three of these secret foundations for a ten-minute magickal meal.

Pasta Power!

Quick to cook, noodles are a mainstay of the ten-minute kitchen witch. Associated with good health and longevity in China, pasta is both wholesome and magickal. It's also very versatile, and you can choose what herbs and vegetables to add to your sauce blends based on the magickal attributes of these ingredients.

To start, fill a pot with water. Hold your hand over the pot and think about the magickal pasta you're about to cook. If it's a joy-inducing spaghetti, conjure an energy of happiness and send this power out of your hand and into the water. If it's defense noodles you're making, summon protective forces to infuse the water with incredible strength. Place the pot on the stove and turn on the burner, invoking the element of fire or calling on the energies of the sun as you do so.

Now grab whatever herbs and/or vegetables you want to use in your recipe and get to washing and chopping and whatever else you need to do to prepare the ingredients for cooking. Make each step of the ingredient preparation process an act of magick, purifying energies as you wash vegetables and fresh herbs, infusing ingredients with your magickal intent as you peel, cut, or tear. Slice vegetables into thin pieces for quicker cooking.

Once the water comes to a boil, put in your noodles. To keep the recipe under ten minutes, choose angel hair pasta or thin spaghetti, and use whole wheat noodles for greater health value and greater magickal power. While the noodles boil, heat a few tablespoons of olive oil in a pan and add any vegetables you're using, then any herbs. Think about the magickal energies of the ingredients you've chosen seeping out into the oil as the heat magnifies their power. Drain the noodles while the vegetables and herbs finish cooking. Once vegetables become bright in color and herbs begin to release their scent, pour the mix over the noodles and toss gently to coat. For a lo mein, add soy sauce. Empower the finished dish with an extra enchantment: think of your magickal goal and send a feeling of success and certainty into the noodles. If you like, affirm out loud the food's purpose, saying something such as, "These joyful noodles will bring happiness to everyone who eats them." Serve and enjoy.

That's a Wrap

Wraps—sandwiches that forgo bread and are instead rolled in tortillas—are a fast, fresh, and fun way to make a magickal meal in no time. Choose vegetables such as yellow squash, zucchini, mushrooms, tomatoes, lettuce, onion, or cucumber. Charm the vegetables to enhance their natural power: simply connect with the energies in the food and call out the attribute most suited to the magick, magnifying the ingredient's inherent qualities or color associations. Prepare the vegetables using a magickal slicing technique, then either put them fresh into the tortilla or quickly saute them in a little butter, letting the heat magnify the magick of your empowered ingredients. Add protein with a bit of cold tofu salad, a nice vegetarian assimilation of chicken salad—just drain a package of firm tofu and mash it up with a little mayonnaise and curry powder. If you're a meat eater, simply add sliced turkey or forkfuls of tuna. Serve rolled in wheat or spinach tortillas, adding cheese or honey mustard if you wish.

Chili to the Rescue!

Another staple of the magickal quick cook is chili, made with canned beans so that it's ready in less than ten minutes. Choose three cans of beans, any combination of dark red kidney beans, light red kidney beans, black beans, garbanzo beans, and pinto beans. All beans are associated with health, prosperity, stability, fertility, growth, increase, and strength. Color attributes can also be considered, perhaps choosing red beans for a meal to bring love, black beans to banish, brown beans for earth energies, and so on. Select the energetic attributes that match your magickal intent and empower the beans you've chosen accordingly, keeping the bean's symbolism and inherent power and the goal of your spellworking in mind as you cook.

All beans are associated with health, prosperity, stability, fertility, growth, increase, and strength. Color attributes can also be considered.

Put the beans in a pot on the stove and set the heat to medium-high. Thinly slice or finely chop any vegetables you plan to use, such as carrots, broccoli, squash, onion, or bell pepper, then add these to the beans, envisioning the magickal energies of the vegetables entering the mix. Add canned tomatoes and stir. Next add spices, empowered to bring out their magick, of course: cumin and garlic for strength, health, and defense; pepper for defensive banishing and binding; salt for purification, protection, and power; and chili powder for magickal energy, banishing, and passion. Stir using Mudra mixing or another magickal technique. Once vegetables are tender and beans are heated, the meal is ready to work its magick.

Prosperity Potatoes

Try this recipe to spark ideas for your own magickal meals.

- 3 small gold potatoes (for tenacity, strength, wealth, or health)
- Pinch of basil (for money or general prosperity)
- Pinch of rosemary (for prosperity or good luck)
- Pinch of salt (for success, prosperity, or energy)
- A few tablespoons of olive oil or other vegetable oil (for wealth)
- 1 can of dark red kidney beans (for strength or passion)

Heat the oil in a pan as you cut the potatoes into very thin slices, thinking of how you are slicing through all obstacles. Place these in the oil and using your hand or wand, trace dollar signs or pentacles over the potatoes. Add the spices as you think about your prosperity growing and wealth pouring down on you from many different channels. Pour in the beans and think of your tenacity and strength.

Let this cook for about seven or eight minutes, until the potatoes are tender, then serve.

. . . .

With just a little practice, you'll quickly master the art of ten-minute magickal cooking and be able to reap the rewards on even your busiest days. You'll increase your ability to direct energy, improve the quality of your food, and have a new effective method for magickally creating the life you desire.

Melanie Marquis's bio appears on page 22.

Illustrator: Christa Marquez

The Sun Also Rises: Dealing with Grief

James Kambos

As I write this piece, summer is at high tide and my garden is filled with color. Yellow coneflowers bloom along the old fence and the hummingbirds look like flying jewels as they flash amid the red bee balm. In the afternoon heat, the cicada's chorus rises—it is the drowsy song of summer.

When a butterfly settles gently on a zinnia, I'm reminded how nature abides by an orderly sense of rhythm. Everything has a purpose and a direction, such as the pattern of the changing seasons.

Yet there inevitably comes a time in each of our lives when we seem to have no purpose and no direction—a time when the only season we know is the season of grief. Such a time came to me recently. A time when I thought the sun would never rise again. This period made me draw upon the wisdom of the Craft more than ever and tested my belief in magic. This is not an article written by an expert. This is only the story of one man's journey out of the darkness, and I'm hoping my experience will help someone else.

Grief is a grim companion that can come to us in various ways. Death, the end of a marriage, and job loss are only a few of the causes. My own grief began after I dealt with a series of tragedies over a short period of time. My boss and friend of twenty-eight years was killed in an automobile collision, so I lost my best friend and my job. The final blow came when my mother, whom I had been caring for the last two years, died unexpectedly.

It was 5 am when I left the hospital the February morning my mother died. The moon was full and frost glinted on the windshields of the cars in the hospital parking lot. I placed my mother's belongings in the backseat. I found it hard to believe she would never need them again.

On the drive home, I experienced my first magical encounter or "sign." As I approached my house, three deer leapt in front of my car. They moved with silent grace in the faint blue light of dawn. Was this a sign from my mother? She had always loved deer, and the number three was symbolic since she had just completed her life cycle of Maiden, Mother, and Crone. As a totem animal, the deer also suggested to me to move cautiously and to trust my intuition.

Weeks later, after the blur of the funeral and dealing with the insurance companies had subsided, I began the hard part: living.

For witches, Pagans, and anyone living a magical life, we have some extra resources to draw upon when dealing with a crisis. It was going to be difficult, but I knew I had to have faith in my spirituality to change my circumstances in a positive way.

You must listen to your inner voice and use your magical system to bring about small victories until you feel that grief is beginning to release its grip on you.

Unfortunately there isn't a spell to completely destroy grief. Instead I found that you must listen to your inner voice and use your magical system to bring about small victories until you feel that grief is beginning to release its grip on you.

What follows is a collection of advice and recommendations, both magical and practical, to help anyone who is finding it difficult to navigate the storm known as grief.

Let the Healing Begin

The hardest part in overcoming grief is taking that first step because you'll have an "I don't care" attitude. Along with pain, you feel a great apathy toward life. That is typical. The first spellwork I performed—and still perform—to relieve myself of grief and depression is speaking an affirmation or a devotional daily.

It doesn't need to be lengthy. Just saying out loud that you're not alone and that your loved one is still with you in some way is a great help. Whether they have passed on or simply passed out of your life, the part they've had in making you the person you are today will never go away. Now is also a good time to thank your guardian spirits for their help. If you're up to it, light a candle on your altar as you do this. At night, thank the Divine Spirit for returning you home safely. If you're mourning the passing of a loved one, don't be surprised if you feel a gentle touch at this time. They *are* close to you.

Dreams can also be important now, although they're not easy for us to control. However, a deceased loved one will most likely contact you during a dream. This can be most comforting. Try to remember the details of the dream because they may contain messages.

USING FOOD AND FRAGRANCE FOR THERAPY

Food is a gift from the Goddess and Mother Earth. During the grieving process, you may lose your appetite, but think of food as a connection to the Life Force itself. This will help.

If you cook, please continue to do so. This will help in two ways. First it will provide nutrition during this critical time; second, the

scent of food cooking will act as a form of aromatherapy. During the dark days following my mother's death, I kept a pot of homemade soup simmering, as its aroma would lift my spirits.

Certain spices, such as cinnamon and nutmeg, have proven to have a similar effect. On days I felt I need a boost (and felt up to the task), I'd bake a pumpkin bread using those spices. As the spicy scent wafted out of my kitchen, I just knew things would get better.

If you're not talented in the kitchen, burn scented candles. Fragrances such as vanilla, apple, spice, and lavender will also help relieve feelings of depression.

Connect with Nature

I have always walked, and even during my darkest days I still took some pleasure in it. Walking will get you outside; you'll smell the earth and begin to really notice the world again. I found myself looking mindfully at the clouds, the trees, and flowers.

Feeding wildlife will help more than you can imagine. I kept my birdfeeders full and squirrel station stocked with corn. Watching the birds and squirrels feed made me realize life continues, and that there is an order to our world.

Most magical people will find solace in gardening during their grieving period. I know I did, even if only for an hour. As I gardened, I realized I was working with a living entity. It grows, it changes, and, yes, it dies—but it also returns. All of these factors reaffirmed my belief in reincarnation, which was a great solace during my period of grieving.

As I gardened, I realized I was working with a living entity. It grows, it changes, and, yes, it dies—but it also returns.

Working with the Tarot

As we grieve, we search for answers. Being a magical person, I turned to my divination tools. My choice was the tarot. I found the visual aspect of the cards to be helpful, as the images frequently mirrored my feelings.

I used a variety of layouts during my readings, and it's interesting to note that some of the same cards would always appear. It was also amazing how the same card would move from the present situation into the future. For example, the Five of Cups, which signifies grieving and loss, was in every spread. Eventually it began to move into the future, in a reversed position. This told me that my feelings of grief would begin to lift. I began to feel hopeful.

Using your favorite divining tool will help you focus and meditate. If you don't feel strong enough to do this work for yourself, perhaps a fellow coven member can help.

RECEIVING HELP

Since many witches belong to covens, the coven would be an ideal place to start if you feel the need of a support group. And if professional help is needed, you can begin by talking to your doctor. He or she will often be able to recommend a local therapist or counselor who specializes in grief or in the specific situation you are facing.

A *note on giving help*: If you know someone who is grieving and you're both part of the magical community, please don't do any type of spellwork without being asked. This could cause bad karma.

A Simple Magical Ritual

This ritual may help ease your pain. Take a walk. As you walk, look for an ordinary stone that appeals to you. Place this stone on your altar. As you meditate about your day, hold this stone. Visualize all your pain entering the stone.

When the day comes that you feel your life is returning to normal, you may get rid of your stone. To do this, go out to a favorite spot, perhaps where you found your stone. Thank the stone, then leave it. Keep walking and don't look back.

. . . .

As I have written this piece, the nights have vibrated with the awesome power that only a summer thunderstorm can possess. Thunder has echoed down the valley and the winds have battered the hills. By sunrise, the world is cleansed. Grief is like that. It pounds away at us and then slowly ebbs, revealing the light. This makes me

realize that there is still an order to everything that happens in our cosmos. There will always be stormy nights, but eventually the sun also rises.

James Kambos *is a writer and artist from Ohio. He spent much of his childhood on his grandparents' Ohio farm, which helped him develop a closeness to nature. His interest in nature continues to influence both his writing and art. His favorite magical tools are the tarot and pendulum.*

Illustrator: Tim Foley

Being Pagan in a Bad Economy

Boudica

Things are tough all over. Thousands are without jobs, laid off, or have had cuts to their hours or salaries. And while everyone seems to be saying we're on the road to recovery, that doesn't hold much water if you're still suffering.

Lack of education, lack of training, and lack of experience are the three biggest barriers that stand between you and your next job. Yes, we can all flip burgers or push carts down at the local big box store, but is that what you really want to do with your life? Is minimum wage going to pay for the clothes on your children's backs, or the food on the table? Do you really want to stand in a line and wait for handouts?

We may be at a starting point to recovery, but this isn't the end. I am going to outline how to get the three things you need to put yourself back into a good-paying job that you may actually enjoy: education, training, and experience.

In *Magick in Theory and Practice* by Aleister Crowley, magick is defined as "the Science and Art of causing Change to occur in conformity with will." This is one of the most profound and yet

Lack of education, lack of training, and lack of experience are the three biggest barriers that stand between you and your new job.

simplest explanations of magick ever. And it establishes very clearly that we all can do magick if we put our Will into it. As they say, where there's a Will, there's a way.

Education

First, how far did you go in school? Did you graduate high school? If not, now is the time to go back and get your GED. It really is not all that hard. There are tutors within the schools and libraries, online, and I bet within your own Pagan community if you ask around. You really need that GED. Most good-paying jobs are just not accessible to you without a diploma. If you are unemployed and drawing an unemployment check right now, go to your local Job and Family Services office and see which schools are offering free GED programs. Also look online. Besides free GED classes in most cities, there are also free practice tests online. Use the magick of the Internet and of the Social Services Department. You can get more lasting help than food stamps and job listings from them if you ask the right questions.

If you have graduated high school, the next step is a college program. Do you know what the Federal Pell Grant is? It is a gift for low-income undergraduates that doesn't have to be repaid. You score big if you are the main provider for a family situation. Federal Pell Grants are big magick if you apply for them.

What? You don't have time to go back to college? Well, yes, actually you do. Besides classes in the college proper, most major colleges (and even some not so major ones) offer online or distance

learning classes you can take from the comfort of your home computer. Teenagers off to school? Go sign in and take a class. Kids off to bed? Go sign in and take a class. Need to take some of your courses in the actual classroom? Schedule a day or evening course, one every semester or quarter. You can also look for lunch

hour tutors if you find yourself needing some face-to-face guidance. Some college students are actually paid to be tutors to nontraditional (older) students, so you will always find someone on your level who will address your educational needs. Or you can search the local bulletin boards for low-cost paid tutors.

The first steps of magick are happening. If you work it just right, the education at this stage of your life will be paid by grants. If you've done military service, now is the best time to cash in on your GI benefits. You should also apply for scholarships. There are scholarships for nontraditional students and for personal needs. There are many kinds of supplementary income opportunities available to the unemployed. You will have to work to find them, though—you'll need to pick the brains of the counselors and social services agencies and discover every opportunity you can. This is the process of magick, the process of change.

Training

So you're back in school, or maybe you are coming up on your last year in school and you encounter the next issue: lack of hands-on training. You know the theories and facts of your chosen professional, but you don't know how to actually *do* it.

Many schools offer programs that partner with local businesses in internship programs, some of which pay a salary (but many do not). Check with your school to see what's available. Whether you think you can do it or not, all they can say is "No." However, persistence pays, and you will eventually find a "Yes."

The next step is to look for a job that may pay you minimum wage to work in your chosen field. Finish school and work part-time in the field you are aspiring to build a career out of. This is a great strategy and I highly recommend it. A part-time job at the entry level will often allow you to do a little bit of everything, giving you some of the best training you can get . . . and a modest income while you're at it. (Editor's note: This editor started in publishing by answering the phone and filing paperwork.)

No one starts out on the top. You have to work up to it, no matter how talented you think you are. This is the "process" of magic, bringing about the change. You are slowly changing yourself. You are improving your chances of landing a good-paying job by working the rituals of education and job skills.

Experience

Entry-level positions with on-the-job training are a "two-fer" bonus. Besides getting the hands-on training that you will need to be good at your job, you also gain job experience. Ask any graduate who has a degree what message they are getting at job interviews, and they will tell you that prospective employers have the pick of the best of the best, and they are going for as much experience as they can get in the given pay scale.

So, again, how do we get real job skills? Taking a job in your chosen field at the entry level is one way. But not all of us live in areas where entry-level jobs are available. Part-time job opportunities are pretty full in my area, as people take whatever jobs they can get in order to earn some kind of paycheck or get in the door of a company they hope will hire them when the job market improves.

But what about the rest of us?

I am going to open a magical door here and make a suggestion that may sound off the wall, but will be a big bonus on your resume if you decide to do it: volunteer.

No matter what you are studying in school, there is an opportunity to volunteer, usually right in your own neighborhood, that will give you an edge in so many ways.

Yes, I know—no pay. Are you receiving an unemployment check right now? Do you have one or two mornings or afternoons a week to give back to your community? That's all it takes to find your way into a place of opportunity to do something that will impress potential employers.

Are you interested in health services? Volunteer at your local hospital. Are you interested in agriculture or horticulture? Volunteer at your local botanical society. Interested in computer programming or IT? Find one of the local 501(c)(3) organizations that offer IT Volunteer/Internships to local college students. Interested in

retail? Volunteer in a store associated with a hospital or any kind of shop attached to a charitable organization. Interested in helping young men or women? Volunteer in a youth organization. There's the Red Cross, the United Way, HIV support organizations, cancer hospices, women's shelters, soup kitchens, public schools, libraries, and children's services. There are secretarial and clerical duties that need to be done for these organizations, as well as educational programs that need volunteers to do outreach to the communities.

Again, these are volunteer positions, which means they offer no pay. But let's examine the benefits: You will be in or near a field you want to work in. You will get on-the-job training. You will often receive verification for the hours you put in, which means you can put this on your resume as experience. And your future employer will be very impressed that you were dedicated enough to give your time and skills to a worthwhile project.

There are grants, scholarships, funding, training, experience, and opportunity out there if you will just take some time to work the magick. Be as diligent at working up a plan and sticking to it as you are with laying out your ritual items. Prepare for the process like you were writing spellwork. Follow through as if Deity were walking beside you with their hand on your shoulder, guiding you through this maze to your final destination.

The final part of working magick is validation. And I can validate this process because it has worked for me and for others. It worked so well that I sponsor a Volunteer Internship Program in my organization for aspiring IT students at the local college. The experience benefits both the students and the organization.

Examine this article and see if there is something that sparks your imagination, see if the magick calls you. Put your feet on a magical path to getting yourself out of this bad economy rut and into something that will benefit you for the rest of your magical life. Make some magick for yourself.

Boudica *is reviews editor and co-owner of* The Wiccan/Pagan Times *and owner of* The Zodiac Bistro, *both online publications. A former New Yorker, she now resides with her husband and eight cats in Ohio.*

Illustrator: Rik Olson

Making the Most of the Moments

Jenett Silver

We all have them—those times when the list of things we want to do is far longer than our resources allow. Sometimes, it's for the best possible reason: we're planning a wedding, having a child, starting school, buying a home, or some other wonderful but big project. At other times, it's for less pleasant reasons: our own health problems, the death of a loved one, the needs of a family member, or long hours at work. It can be easy to feel too overwhelmed for magical practice at

the exact time when we most need and want support from our religious and magical work.

What's even harder is that a change in one part of life often triggers change in other parts. A schedule change may affect when we can see our friends or what events we can attend. Someone who is facing constant exhaustion may need to adjust their meditation practice or how they handle their own energy work. Someone who is the caretaker for a loved one may not have much uninterrupted time for rituals.

Challenges also change how we see ourselves. Someone who does a lot of writing, reading, or creative work can find it hard to adapt if they can't concentrate or focus for long. Someone who loves larger group events can be just as upset if their health, available time, or energy limit their attendance. Some people find that health issues or medications change how they perceive and work with magical energy. If we've been active in our community, we might also worry about what others will think of us if we don't continue to take on a particular task or attend all the same events. We may be forced to take a break from a group or practice we truly enjoy.

The good news is that we can choose how we face our busy challenges by choosing to use all the tools available to us—including magic and ritual—to help ourselves through the hard times, and to help make sure we remain focused on what we truly care about and need. This article outlines ways to help ourselves do just that, as well as ways to share our experience of these hard times with others when we need a little extra help and support.

Take Time For Reflection

It's easy to get tangled in the complexity of change. We forget to step back and look at the whole of our life—all the things that go into making our lives rich and full and meaningful to us. One easy way to avoid this is to find some time for reflection when we first start to sense that changes are in the air. Some people like sitting down and talking through changes with a close friend. Some people like writing in a journal. You might like to try a divination reading to help you focus your attention, or meditation or ritual to help guide you to the areas that need your attention most. Fundamentally, though, you just need yourself, some time, and some questions.

1) What makes you happy and feeds your dreams?

Our joys and passions are important, especially during challenging times. For some people, it's creative work; for others, spending time with family, gardening, or another hobby. Write a list of the things you enjoy. Some items will take more time, energy, and focus than others. Brainstorm ways you can include these things in your life. If you enjoy music, listening to music has different demands on you than playing or writing it. You might enjoy cooking, but find that easy slow cooker meals fit your new schedule and energy level much better than preparing a fresh seven-course meal.

2) What must you do?

Obviously, it's important to take care of our basic needs. That means everything from sleep and food to paying your bills. And for most of us, that means work. While we don't always have a lot of control over the details of our work environment, there are often simple practical things we can do that can save our time and energy for other things. Perhaps changing how we get to work would cause less stress, take less time, or allow us to read or listen to music on the way. Maybe bringing our lunch would help us eat in a way that better supported our health. Maybe taking time to find a quiet corner and read or listen to music during a break would let us recharge. Perhaps going for a walk outside on break would be of more benefit than ten minutes spent surfing the Internet. Long term, be open to changes, maybe in what you do or where you work, that would better support your dreams. If you work in front of a computer, try evoking the different elements and their energies to balance yourself while you do what you need to do. Use pictures of an ocean or river for watery calm, a cozy campfire or hearth for fiery energy, a wind chime or streamers for airy inspiration, or smooth stones for earthy grounding. Or just put up a photo or desktop background that reminds you to relax and take a deep breath.

The same thing goes for home. Someone has to do the dishes, laundry, and other cleaning. However, a clear look at how we're doing those things helps us find a great solution. Look at all the tasks you're currently doing: do they all need to happen that often? If you live with others, check in about chore preferences. You might find out that one person hates doing dishes and would be glad to swap that task for something you dislike or find especially tiring.

If you live alone, consider whether your budget could stretch to occasional cleaning help for the chores you really struggle with, or invite a friend over to talk while you do the task. This will keep you on track to stick to the task but distracted by your friend. Don't be afraid to look for unusual solutions, either. I don't have a dishwasher and kept putting off doing the dishes because I hated washing glasses by hand. I then decided to replace the glasses with ceramic mugs, which I actually enjoy washing. (And if I drop one, they're much easier to clean up.) The point is to find ways to do what you have to do while either incorporating something you enjoy or lessening the time it takes to do it.

3) What time and energy is left?

Take out your calendar and list everything you need to do in an average week, including work (and your commute), household chores, meals, your shower or bath, and enough sleep. If you're dealing with medical issues, factor in plenty of time for rest. Once you have your average week, look at the time you have left. A good rule of thumb is to plan events to take up about 80 percent of your available time so you have some flexibility. That means that some things you've been doing may not fit in your life right now. You'll get more enjoyment out of one ritual where you are fully present than three where your mind is distracted by all the other stuff you need to get done. You can choose events that fit well in your calendar (at times you don't have other commitments), or you might choose to have a busier Tuesday than you'd like, but leave Monday and Wednesday open, so you have plenty of time to prepare and recover.

4) Are there any other considerations?

A number of life events—grief, many medical conditions, medication, a new baby—can make us feel like we're moving through a thick fog for months, right at a time when we most need to focus. There are lots of great resources out there for time management and

handling commitments. A good starting place is David Allen's book *Getting Things Done: The Art of Stress-Free Productivity* (Penguin, 2002), but a search on "productivity" online will turn up lots of other options. Another good term is "lifehacking," commonly used for tips and tricks that save time and energy in varied ways. Take a bit of time to research how you can save yourself time. That way you won't have to think about time management when you've had a crazy day.

5) Who should you tell about the changes in your life?

When your life changes in any significant way, a good rule of thumb is to tell anyone who would notice: telling them means you can help them understand what's going on without guessing (and possibly coming to the wrong conclusion). If you need to see friends less than you'd like, telling them why will help them understand and not take offense. If you're working with a magical or religious group or teacher, it's also good to talk to them and figure out the best options for everyone. Consider finding a group of people who are dealing with similar issues or situations. There are lots of support group options (both online and offline) that can help you with specific, practical issues around caregiving, parenting, or chronic illness. Many Pagan forums also have spaces for people with specific interests to share ideas and support one another. These resources are fantastic because they help you learn from what other people do, so you don't have to reinvent the wheel for yourself.

As you get more experience with the changes your life has gone through, you'll also get a sense of which things still need adjustment. For example, I've enjoyed the Pagan camping festivals I've been to, but they take a lot out of me, not only the time of the festival, but extra planning beforehand to make sure I'll be able to enjoy myself and have lots of recovery time afterward. These days, I'd rather spend my time in other ways, so I help create less-intense events or choose to see people at local one-day events that don't put the same demands on my health.

Interweave Magic

Once you've taken the time to sort out the bigger pieces of your life, it's time to take a look at how you can weave magic and religious practice into your life in ways that help you, not drain you.

Creating an altar or shrine is an ongoing way to remind yourself of your goals and important deity or magical relationships. You might create one to honor a particular deity, to focus on healing, or to help with any other goal or desire in your current life. You might choose to have several smaller shrines in different rooms with different goals. A shrine does not need to be elaborate: a few small items are often just as effective for keeping you mindful as a large and elaborate shrine. Think through the upkeep: fresh flowers take more care than a houseplant that only needs occasional water.

Seasonal altars can be lovely, but if you don't always have the energy to change them promptly, they might be more distressing than helpful. Tarot or other divination deck cards can be a great and easy way to bring a specific focus to a shrine (by picking an appropriate card for your focus), as can other pieces of art.

A related practice is wearing jewelry. This doesn't need to be limited to a pentacle or another obviously magical symbol: any piece of jewelry that's meaningful to you will work. Most of my jewelry comes from small independent jewelry-makers, and each piece has a particular focus for me. I might wear one on a day that I want balance and grace, another on a day when I need a little extra patience, yet another when I could use some extra healing. Simply reaching up and running my fingers over the piece (or just feeling the weight around my neck) helps me remember what my real goals for the day are, which can help immensely.

Music and other things you listen to can also be a great way to include your magical and ritual life throughout your busy day. Computers, phones, and mp3 players often have applications that allow you to select music for an alarm (or there's the older method of a mix CD in your clock/radio.) Even if you choose a louder alarm, you can still put the music on while you're getting ready for the day, and choose music that will help you keep your focus on your goals and the things that help you start the day with a smile.

Consider taking time every day for a little reading, as well as some listening. You might choose to read a few interesting blogs before you start your day, or you could bring a book with you to read over lunch or while waiting for things to get started at a meeting. If you'd rather not bring something witchy with you, you can pick fiction or non-fiction that still fits in with your goals and interests in some other way. I'm really fond of microhistories (those books about a single subject like salt, color, honey, or many other topics) for this: I always pick up fascinating folklore and history that then gets tied back into my magical practice. If reading is too tiring for you, podcasts, audio books, and movies might all work better for you, letting you enjoy learning something new or be carried along with a powerful story that helps you along your path as well. Audiobooks from your local library can be a great way to make commute time more useful and enjoyable. Most libraries have a good audio collection of fiction and classics, but you might need to search online if you want specifically Pagan books.

Food is another great way to tap into your magical and religious practice. If time and energy are at a premium, you might not be up for a lot of cooking, but there are quick and easy ways to add things in. (See Melanie Marquis' article on page 66 for some quick ideas.) One of my friends introduced me to the idea of "opportunity food"—those things that are quick and easy to make, but still nutritious and filling. It's easy to add a seasoning herb with magical intention to a can of soup you're heating, or add a few herbs to prepared pasta sauce, even if you're not up to making it from scratch. Do the same thing with what you're drinking, too. It's easy to stir a little healing into a mug of tea or a little extra love into a mug of cocoa or spiced cider—try honey, cinnamon, or nutmeg. You can also try cooking large portions of freezable foods when you feel better or have a bit more time. You can then pull them out on the days when time and energy have completely run out—homemade food without the homemade fuss.

If your time and energy are limited, it may be a bad time to attempt lots of major magical work. Instead, focus on building your magical and ritual work around those things you need to do anyway. Including a simple energy cleansing ritual in your bathing routine doesn't add time and can help you feel better. You can pick soaps or additions that help you keep your goals in mind—rosemary for healing from illness, rose for blessing yourself, even products that include coffee or citrus to help you wake up in the morning. Some people find it helpful to offer the work of tending their home or their children to a particular deity associated with those things; others do the same thing with tending a pet or a garden. Say a blessing before each meal. Add a short cleansing ritual to your dish washing. Experiment with other practices, like a daily devotion, but don't be rigid. If you can't keep it up, look for alternatives that fit your current needs better. This is an area where ideas and help from others can be especially helpful.

. . . .

While each of these by itself is a small and fairly simple step, added together, they can provide many options to keep your personal path vibrant during a time when changes in your life mean longer rituals or activities may not be practical. Follow a few of these tips and you'll see that you can indeed live a busy, but magical life.

Jenett Silver *is priestess of a small coven in Minneapolis, Minnesota. A librarian and general geek, she's also deeply familiar with the challenges of competing demands, chronic health issues that can't be ignored, and all the other things that go into a complex life. You can find more of her writing on the web on her blog at http://gleewood.org/threshold.*

Illustrator: Bri Hermanson

Starting a New Moon Group

Gail Wood

In ancient times, the Hebrew tribes waited patiently on hilltops for darkness to change. Once the new moon showed her first tiny sliver of light, they lit signal fires, sounded trumpets and ran to the villages telling all that the light of the moon had returned. In observance of this new moon, women were exempted from work and household responsibilities. This is a minor Jewish holiday called Rosh Chodesh, meaning "head of the month."

Today, Judaism follows a lunar calendar and the beginning of the month

The velvety dark sky
shimmers
And opens its arms
To welcome Her
A tiny sliver of light.
Sharp, silver crescent
Herald of beginnings
Emerging from darkness.
New moon, bright moon.
Inspire, renew, and
delight.
Hail and welcome!

is announced in observances and synagogues. Women formed Rosh Chodesh groups and gathered together during the Rosh Chodesh. These groups had many purposes, including to study and learn. Many of these groups focus on Shekinah (the feminine force of God) and the role of womanhood in religious and contemporary life. These groups had a great resurgence in the 1970s and many still exist today. Each group is different and individual. One group's older women may guide the younger women in discovery on various topics such as sexuality, body issues, and spiritual topics. Other groups may gather to share their lives and pursue topics of interest and projects.

From ancient times to the present, from ancient Hebrew tradition to modern Pagan womanhood, the new moon is celebrated as a time to start new things, learn new things, and begin the cycle of life anew. In a busy world, a new moon group can provide women with a space of time to share their lives and explore new things. It's a wonderful time to bring old issues to a close and to open the door to new opportunities.

Starting a group and maintaining its momentum takes some planning and a time commitment; with that commitment come great rewards in sisterhood, community, and a deep understanding of Spirit. Every good, sustainable plan starts with an idea, a spark of inspiration, followed by ongoing commitment and adaptability. What follows are some ideas and advice on starting and sustaining a new moon group. There is only one unchanging rule: it should be fun and it should matter to you.

The Idea

Inspired by the new moon, you begin with a fresh idea to start a group, to gather together when the moon is new. Begin by thinking about your purpose. Is it to learn, to create sisterhood, or to deepen your understanding of spiritual things? It could be all of these or some other reason. Having a clear, mutual understanding of your purpose helps keep the group centered and focused when the weather gets bad, when life intervenes, and when the group goes through its growing pains. My advice is to stay clear and focused, to start small, and to be practical and flexible.

You might want to establish a name for your group. A name can be very simple such as The New Moon Group or another name rooted in your mutual vision or idea. A name helps to develop the group mind. A local group in my area is named the Merry Elementals. Their commitment is to learn together, honor the elemental energy, and not take themselves too seriously. Their gatherings and their group mind reflect their deep understanding of air, water, earth, fire, and spirit and they are, indeed, merry. They laugh a lot

and through their commitment, they are present for each other in good times and in bad times.

Making the Commitment and Establishing a Calendar

Once your idea and vision burn clear and bright, make a commitment to keep the group going for an established time period. It can be a quarter, a year-and-a-day in the tradition of the witches of old, or some other time period. As part of your commitment, you will want to establish meeting times and develop a calendar of meetings dates. New moon dates can be a challenge since the calendar of dates in our daily lives is a solar calendar. The new moon moves to different days of the week. I was in a new moon group that wanted to meet exactly on the night of the new moon each month. The date became sort of a floating holiday decided by the hostess. It became too great a challenge for five busy women to be available every new moon. The group finally faded away because there was never enough notice and the date floated too freely. It wasn't practical. A more successful group has been one that chose a specific day of the week and then gathered on that day closest to the moon phase. It's easier to count on having a meeting on the Friday nearest the new moon than on the actual new moon date.

Attendance and Rules

For most of us, rules remind us of our work-a-day world, and one of the things we want to do in our group is be set apart from those kinds of details. Often, rules and guidelines can involve punishment and reward. But it doesn't have to be like that. We can shift our attitude to look at taking care of this kind of detail as establishing a framework for all the wonderful discoveries our group is going to make. Once in place, the framework can take care of itself with some maintenance from time to time. This kind of framework can give the group member a safe harbor to explore who they are and discover more about themselves and the magical world of the moon.

As part of the commitment to the group, you may wish to establish guidelines for attendance. This is all a matter of personal choice and part of the vision. For instance, if you want some consistency, you may need to have a core number of people who attend all or most of the time. As the leader of a group, I made a commitment to establish the calendar and attend every meeting. I did begin to develop a back-up plan in case I ever needed to be elsewhere and could not attend. One of my proudest moments occurred when I had to be out of town for a family illness and a major ritual was to happen at the same time. Our back-up plans went into place and the ritual and meeting occurred; it was fabulous. I was able to be there in spirit while I was physically where I most needed to be.

There are other rules you may wish to establish. The most effective ones are those that are made together, a sort of agreement developed around your core purpose. Guidelines for confidentiality, inviting guests, communication, various courtesies, tardiness, time, and expenses are all issues groups end up grappling with. How is leadership handled and how are decisions made? Are there areas that are considered "no trespassing?" Are those kinds of taboos acceptable? Be sure to allow time for chatter, follow-up, and check-in, and allow for people to slough off the cares of their day.

It's human nature to establish some rules and guidelines and then forget to update them as things evolve. Pick a time, perhaps at the beginning of the year or the birthday of your group, to go over your guidelines. That keeps your understanding and awareness of the process fresh and clear. This also builds in an ongoing and healthy attitude of adaptation and informal evaluation.

To make gatherings meaningful so that you and others look forward to meetings requires a little bit of thought. Keep what you explore simple and personal. There's no need to create a book-sized handout for each meeting and deliver a lecture worthy of Sister Mary Margaret from your schooldays. Something interesting that is well presented, explored, discussed, and learned will keep people coming back and will keep you engaged and empowered.

Gatherings: Ritual Aspects

Now comes the fun part—planning and having your new moon group meet. Some of the nicest groups I've attended were friendly and casual with very little ritual formalities. That doesn't mean that rituals are absent, it means the ritual elements are less ceremonial. Attention to spirit in whatever form is chosen becomes part of the heartbeat of the group. In one group, the women had a very nice large candle in a beautiful holder. They lit it, chanting the same words every time. At the end of their gathering, they extinguished it while chanting a parting sentiment. The candle and its holder traveled home with the hostess of the next gathering. Their meetings consisted of a lesson or a craft, a lot of laughter, and really good food.

Food is an important part of spiritual gatherings. I have wonderful memories of some incredible church suppers. Covered dish, dish-to-pass, and potluck are regional terms for a gathering where people bring food! It's an amazing way to establish community, share stories and history, and make new stories—all created through our food and unique recipes!

Food is important to women and women's groups. Most of us in this media-saturated world have grown up with a complex relationship with both our body and food. I think men look at food in a completely different way than women; for the most part, they see it as a pleasure and as a necessity. For women, food is much more complicated. Food can be both positive and negative. In its negative form, food can be a weapon or a punishment; in the positive state, the food we prepare is our way of nurturing—it's a gift and expression of love and healing to those we love. Food can be a comfort and a friend when times are sad and difficult. Food is communion, a way to establish and maintain community, a way to communicate, and sometimes an avenue to the difficult stories and confessions

about body and family issues. Food is nurturing, food is communication, and food can be an expression of love. Still, food can also be extremely negative. So in spiritual groups, we walk a fine line with food. Be sensitive to the needs of your members when it comes to food and drink.

However, many times, food is just food. With your group, make a commitment to regard food as a delight and a gift. As the Charge of the Goddess tells us, "all acts of love and pleasure are my rituals." Seek to make food for your sisters as a generous portion of delicious, delightful tastes and satisfaction of appetites. Make a promise to yourself to enjoy the food at your gatherings. Food is also symbolic of the bounty of the green earth, the generosity of Mother Earth.

What to Explore?

It's always a challenge to find and implement ideas for a group meeting. Having a cache of ideas to delve into can help keep the inspiration fresh and the ideas flowing. When I was teaching, other teachers and I used to joke that we only needed to keep "one chapter ahead." While that seems ill-prepared, it isn't really. Being prepared and ready ahead of time alleviates the stress of last-minute preparation and the fear that your muse of inspiration might desert you. I always keep a handy list of topics and themes I want to explore. As leader, I feel I learn as much as (or more than) anyone else in the group.

Since this is a new moon group and the moon is sacred to so many goddesses, consider having a Goddess of the Month to learn about or to be a "sponsor." For one year, I had a Divine Sponsor for our meeting each month. I wrote a charge of the goddess or god as part of what I called, "and now a word from our sponsors." You can approach this in a variety of ways, including a lesson, having each member reflect on what that goddess means to them, or sharing objects and food sacred to her. Every culture in the world has moon goddesses. Diana was the maiden goddess of the crescent moon to the Romans, as was Artemis to the Greeks. In Egypt, Bast, Isis, Hagar, and Nephtys were all goddesses of the moon. There's seven right there!

The moon in all phases is a celestial body prominent in astrological thinking. Each month, you can learn more about the zodiac signs and your relationship to them. Strive to go deeper than the just the facts of dates, elements, associations, and qualities to make the understanding personal. You might want to key the topic to what sign the new moon is in. Here are some possible themes for the astrological year of new moon groups:

Aries is a cardinal fire sign. It is action-oriented and responds quickly and with determination. Aries is the spark of inspiration.

Taurus is a fixed earth sign. It is loyal, steadfast, and practical. Taurus can endure much and manifests dreams and desires.

Gemini is a mutable air sign. It is intellect and thinking, and it craves variety. Gemini is communication and mental effort.

Cancer is a cardinal water sign. It is nurturing, home-making, and nest-building. Cancer is sensitive, caring, and intuitive.

Leo is a fixed fire sign. It is romantic, affectionate, and confident. Leo is entertaining, in-charge, and ambitious.

Virgo is a mutable earth sign. It is analytical, organized, and craves perfection. Virgo is thorough, reliable, and cautious.

Libra is a cardinal air sign. It is companionable, with a strong sense of fair play. Libra seeks justice, sees both sides, and is social.

Scorpio is a fixed water sign. It seeks to unravel mysteries and has strong will and intense drives. Scorpio is intense and resourceful.

Sagittarius is a mutable fire sign. It is optimistic and easygoing and loves freedom. Sagittarius is humorous, philosophical, and spiritual.

Capricorn is a cardinal earth sign. It is organized, practical, and hard working. Capricorn is methodical, loyal, and self-disciplined.

Aquarius is a fixed air sign. It is independent, eccentric, and helpful. Aquarius sees the big picture.

Pisces is a mutable water sign. It is imaginative, dreamy, and artistic. Pisces is sensitive and psychic.

Our Western astrological system is based on a solar calendar, but it is also not the only astrological system out there. The thirteen-month Celtic Lunar calendar is based on trees and has animals and qualities assigned to them. The months are Birch, Rowan, Ash, Alder, Willow, Hawthorn, Oak, Holly, Hazel, Vine, Ivy, Reed, and Elder. The Chinese zodiac is based on animals and provides a number of qualities to explore each month. The twelve animals are rat, ox, tiger, rabbit, dragon, snake, horse, sheep, monkey, rooster, dog, and boar (pig).

Divination systems also provide a rich resource of learning and exploration. Tarot, runes, I-Ching, pendulums, and divination of ordinary objects are all resources for your group. The possibilities are endless!

All of these systems have many ancient and contemporary ideas associated with them. They can provide you and your group with a rich well of ideas. You can take these themes as a springboard for your gathering. Remember that these are just suggestions, part of your tool kit for creating a great monthly group meeting.

How to Explore Your Themes

Once you have a sense of the topic or topics you want to pursue, how do you pursue it? How do you make it meaningful and helpful to everyone in the group? Be sure to take in your sisters' thoughts and find out what they are yearning for. Draw on their expertise. Perhaps one is a wonderful singer; another might be a healer, a dancer, or writer. Or perhaps they need to be encouraged to think of themselves as knowledgeable women of power and talent. Sometimes it's all in feeling comfortable or safe in exploring a new side of yourself.

There are a number of ways to explore topics, and sometimes your themes might even help you find a way to explore. In one group, we all created our own individual rune system using symbols from our respective lives and our mutual group mind. To me, that was a much more effective way of understanding runes than using a manufactured set of runes. Another time, we meditated on what we knew of the Tarot and created a card that would represent ourselves.

Another approach is to explore different meditation techniques in relationship to the theme. Perhaps breath meditation during a meeting exploring air or an air sign, shamanic drumming and power allies during a meeting exploring the Chinese zodiac, or time spent creating chants, writing, or dancing. There are lots of possibilities.

While all of this is fun and meant to be fun, many of the revelations can be intense, sad, or even heart-breaking. By building in solid techniques for grounding, checking in, and releasing these energies, you can make sure that the intensity doesn't become disastrous. Sometimes it's as simple as providing a tissue; other times, it's being there with a listening ear, a grounding meditation, or a shoulder to cry on.

A long time ago, I was part of a religious study group. After each lesson, we each came up with an application, something the lesson brought to the foreground that we would carry with us and use in the world. It could be very simple. One of mine was based on the

preciousness of water, and my application was to turn off the water as I brushed my teeth. It honored the earth, the gods, and me. Developing an application from the lesson became a transformative way to make sure we didn't just forget information from meeting to meeting—a way to remember that the lessons we learned were meaningful and would change our lives. Encouraging people to think in this way can be as simple as asking what their application of the lesson might be. During the next meeting's check-in session, follow up on those applications.

A new moon group will ebb and flow just as the moon herself does. At some time you may need to end the group or change its form. Remember: the moon calls the waves to rise and fall in rhythm with her wisdom. Seek the joy of her love and reflect it in your own sense of fun and belonging.

Gail Wood *has been sewing and embroidering since the second grade. She comes from a long line of practical women who sewed, quilted, and knitted as an expression of love and a way to stretch the budget. She has been a priestess of Wicca for more than 25 years. She can be reached at darkmoonwitch@earthlink.net or through her website at www.rowdy goddess.com.*

Illustrator: Kathleen Edwards

The Art of Magickal
Care Packages

Blake Octavian Blair

We live in a time when we have the ability to send communication at the touch of a finger through technology such as email and text message. But sometimes a bit more personal and tangible touch is called for. We like to know that others are thinking of us not only in times of need, but also just because they care. This is why sending magickal care packages can be such a joy and a great form of reaching out to foster and strengthen a sense of community, both locally and beyond.

The reasons to send a magickal care package are as numerous as the items you can include in them. Your reason for sending the package will help you determine what to include in the parcel. At this point, you may be asking yourself, "What exactly makes a care package magickal?" The answer is, of course, *you*! The energies and intentions you put into the process of choosing, creating, gathering, and packing the items create a great amount of magickal energy.

Let's take a look at some of the reasons you might send a magickal care package to someone, as well as a few ideas of what kind of items you may choose to include. One of the most obvious reasons would be to send well wishes and healing energy to a person recovering from an illness, medical condition, or surgery. Other ailments can include the loss of loved ones (animal or human), the loss of one's job, or if a person you know is going through a particularly rough emotional patch. As witches we are well aware of the effectiveness of sending directed healing energy, and a care package is a tangible

manifestation of this power. A wonderful inclusion in this type of package would be a candle that has been anointed with a healing oil such as lavender or eucalyptus, carved with healing symbols, and charged with healing energy. Perhaps one could also employ their kitchen witch skills to bake the person a batch of scrumptious lavender cookies, visualizing their healing during the baking process. Other items that lend themselves well to healing packages include crystals and gemstones that correspond to the ailment and area of the body that is in need of healing, such as bloodstone for the circulatory system/heart/kidneys or labradorite for problems relating to the digestive tract. Clear quartz crystals can be programmed with any intent you wish. Let's also not forget that healing and soothing teas like green tea and chamomile tea make an excellent gift.

The acquisition of a new home is another wonderful opportunity to let your loved ones know you're thinking of them. A person's home is their sanctuary, refuge, and temple. Creating a magickal housewarming package can be especially fun as you choose items to help lend your blessings to this person's new home. House cleansing and blessing items such as sage smudge bundles, sweet grass braids, or a homemade protection/house blessing incense are all wonderful ideas. A horseshoe to hang over the door for protection, luck, and prosperity would be a charming and thoughtful addition as well. When my partner and I moved into our current home, we were sent a care package by a coven of dear friends. It included a hand drawn sigil for blessing and protection, an herb and candle spell kit for setting up wards and protecting our new home, and a CD of relaxation music and baked goods infused with love. It was a loving and thoughtfully planned parcel designed to help us bless, protect, and settle into our new home.

Handfastings and weddings are another great reason to send a package. Inspiration can be drawn from many sources for items to include in this type of care package. A possible theme to keep in mind during the creation of this package is that of pairs. Things that come in twos will serve as a symbol of the union the two being joined will soon enter into. Items the couple may need for their ceremony may also be great gifts to include in the package. These can easily be determined by talking to those being handfasted. Perhaps you can gift them with the perfect set of chalices or a wonderful piece of statuary to sit on their handfasting altar. When my partner and I were handfasted, we received a handfasting care package from friends that included a carefully and specially handmade blend of handfasting incense. Even though these friends could not attend the ceremony due to distance, they were able to make a very special contribution as the lovely scent filled the ritual space during the ceremony.

When I lived in Florida, our local Pagan community started a program to send care packages to Pagan soldiers participating in a Pagan group on an army base in Iraq. Although we are now thankfully reaching a time when the U.S. military is recognizing Pagan and Wiccan paths, Pagan soldiers are still in great need and are deeply appreciative of acknowledgement and contact from their Pagan brothers and sisters on the homefront. When sending packages to military groups overseas, it is important to check beforehand what types of items are permitted—both the military and the postal service have guidelines and restrictions as to what type of items may be sent. Items that were popular among the recipients of our packages included divination tools such as tarot decks and pendulums, pentacle pendants and other magickal jewelry, as well as metaphysical books of all kinds, both new and used. Altar tools and even ritual items were also readily accepted, giving a much-needed (even if small) touch of the sacred to a harsh working environment. With these packages we included several seemingly mundane items that take on a magickal meaning when given with love due to how much they were needed and sought after by the soldiers. Things like drink mix packets, shelf-stable snack foods, playing cards, and old magazines to pass the time. However, in the soldier care packages, the most requested and coveted items were heartfelt handwritten letters. Even to a stranger, sharing the normalcy of life back at home can bring great grounding and comfort. You'd be surprised how interested a deployed soldier may be in hearing about the simple ritual

… in soldier care packages, the most requested and coveted items were heartfelt handwritten letters.

you did with your family for a sabbat. On a similar note, there are many growing Pagan and Wiccan prison ministries as well. These individuals would also benefit from care packages, for many of the same reasons. Remember to check before sending, as with the military packages, to see what items are permitted.

You might also consider sending a friend a solar return package. A person's solar return happens on or very close to their birthday, marking the occasion when the sun returns to the same position it was in at the time of their birth. Think of this type of package as a kit for an enchanting birthday celebration. Suns and celestial-themed items make great additions; plan in advance and keep your eye out for items like cosmic-themed candles or holders or similar items, as stores shift their seasonal merchandise toward the start of the summer season. Stained glass sun catchers to hang in the window also make for a creative solar tie-in. And by all means, include any of the normal birthday trappings you would normally want to send along, such as a card or gift (with your own magickal touches of course).

• • • • • • • • • • • • •

With any type of magical package, keep in mind that shopping locally (rather than in a large chain store) and supporting fair trade is highly preferable, both in terms of karma and in the uniqueness of the items themselves.

As mentioned earlier, a major component of what actually makes a magickal care package magickal is the energy and intent you put into its creation. This includes the packing materials you use. As a general rule of thumb, we witches generally like to be as respectful and gentle as we can to our Mother Earth. To lower your impact, consider re-purposing boxes, bubble wrap, and other packing materials. Be creative when choosing your supplies. A creative friend once sent me a package in the fall and used fallen autumn leaves he

gathered from his yard as the padding material. It added quite an enchanting seasonal touch! Also, boxes you receive through the mail can often easily be re-used numerous times. If it proves difficult to cover previous mailing labels or printing on the box, simply recycle a brown paper bag to wrap the box. This provides a lovely clean canvas to extend your magick to the package's exterior through the use of magickal runes, symbols, and sigils. You can keep the energy flowing and help protect your package right up through its arrival to the recipient through the use of spellcraft. One can draw a rune such as *raidho* or another symbol that corresponds to safe travel (such as Mercury) on the outside of the package, and even recite an incantation for it, such as, "Swiftly traveling through the nation, may this parcel safely reach it's destination. So mote it be!" It never hurts to add a little bit of magickal insurance to your mail. If you include something quite valuable, purchase mundane insurance as well!

One of my favorite personal touches to spruce up envelopes when sending or including a letter or card within a package is to use a sealing wax stamp. This effectively, through both intent and action, seals your letter or card's intent as it would in a spell. And wax seals have such a charming antiquarian feel to them.

It is wonderfully fun to set up a care package exchange with magickal friends. Exchanges can be arranged in a variety of ways. One arrangement is to simply periodically send each other packages in turn. A more structured method would be to exchange packages on each sabbat. Yule would naturally lend itself to such an exchange; however, creatively themed packages can be derived for any of the other sabbats as well. Mutually arrive at an exchange arrangement that works for all parties involved. Remember, this should be a fun project and not a source of undue stress.

The reasons for sending care packages and creating exchanges extend well beyond the actual occasions we send them for. A care package exchange is a welcome way to attract abundance into your life and the lives of others. The Law of Attraction will be automatically set into play, and simply by sharing and putting your intentions out in the world, you'll be welcoming those same energies to return to you.

Care packages are a great way to cultivate and strengthen community bonds. Perhaps you have magickal friends who live in rural areas with very little in-person community fellowship. In this day and age, it's also not uncommon to have people whom you consider part of your spiritual family living many thousands of miles away from you. It is for these reasons that "just because" is reason enough to send someone a care package. As Pagans we tend to form our own sacred tribes. Anyone who has found themselves a part of such a tribe knows the bond of community holds a magick all its own—and that knows no geographical bounds. Nothing says "I care and wish to include you as part of my community" more than a spontaneous package in the mail for no reason other than the fact that you were fondly thought of. Through care packages, we also have the ability to be with loved ones in spirit when we may not be able to be there in person for occasions such as graduations, weddings, initiations, childbirths, and other milestones or rites of passage.

> **A care package exchange is a welcome way to attract abundance into your life and into the lives of others. The Law of Attraction will be automatically set into play.**

When a care package project is taken on at a coven or community level, it can serve as a wonderful community-building activity. Decide within your group whose strengths lie where and what items each person could contribute. Everyone has something to offer, it's just a matter of deciding what to include. If you have adept kitchen witches, they can commit to contribute baked items. Perhaps you have an artisan skilled in sculpture and pottery who may make a mug to include in the package. If you have a knitter in the group, a pair of cozy socks or mittens knitted with caring intent would be a great addition. The package is now not only well on its way to being the perfect assemblage to make someone very cozy and loved on a cool autumn or winter night, but in turn your group has worked closely together to make this happen for the recipient or recipients. You can see how care package exchanges bring the *entire* community closer together—the sending party gains just as much as the receiving party.

Blake Octavian Blair *is an Eclectic IndoPagan Witch, psychic, tarot reader, freelance writer, energy worker, and a devotee of Lord Ganesha. He holds a degree in English and religion from the University of Florida. Blake lives in the Piedmont Region of North Carolina with his beloved husband, an aquarium full of fish, and an indoor jungle of houseplants. Visit him on the web at www.blakeoctavianblair.com or write him at blake@blake octavianblair.com.*

Illustrator: Christa Marquez

Witchcraft Essentials

PRACTICES, RITUALS & SPELLS

Dancing the Morris: Where Old Meets New

Chandra Moira Beal

It's May Day in the Cotswold region of England, and a group of middle-aged, bearded men wearing white stockings and green sashes are dancing in a circle, waving handkerchiefs. They are dancing the Morris. Down on the south coast, another group of dancers weaves in and out of a circle. They are young men and women, dressed all in black, including their faces. Some of them wield sticks that they bang together rhythmically. They are also Morris dancing.

For the past century, Morris dancing has been mainly the domain of older

English men partial to traditional costume and drinking bitter beer. However, a new group of dancers is emerging and bringing with them elements of Goth, Paganism, and a swirl of modern values.

Morris dancing is a distinct English folk tradition, usually performed in groups, that involves stepping in rhythm and choreographed dance. Dancers may use sticks, swords, and handkerchiefs to accentuate their movements. Music is provided by a pipe and tabor or a fiddle, or more commonly, a melodeon. Accordions and concertinas may also be heard, and drums are often employed.

The dance got its name from its origin in the Moorish sword dance, which was devised to celebrate the unification of Spain in the fifteenth century with the driving out of the Moors. Dances with similar names were performed all over Europe and eventually reached the shores of Britain, where they evolved into a dance of the peasantry, performed especially at Whitsun (also known as Pentecost, seven weeks after Easter). Morris dancing was considered too sensual by the puritan seventeenth-century protectorate Oliver Cromwell, and so was suppressed. His successor, King Charles II,

revived it. Although modern Morris dancing contains many Pagan elements, there is actually no evidence that it is a pre-Christian ritual.

Dancing the Morris retained popularity until the Industrial Revolution, at which point many of the "country" customs were abandoned. The traditions, however, were kept quietly alive by English folklorists, who recorded first the music and later the dance steps. Some believe these recordings were selective and weeded out the sensual or dark elements of the dance, leaving a sanitized version to survive. Several men's teams, or sides, were formed in the early twentieth century, based on this version, and an explosion of new dance teams, some of them women's or mixed sides, appeared during the folk revival of the 1960s and 1970s.

Morris dancing continues in modern Britain, with exhibitions commonly seen at country fairs and holidays. There are around 150 teams in the United States, and there are many sides in the Commonwealth countries of Australia, Canada, New Zealand, and Hong Kong. Isolated groups exist in other countries, such as Holland, Sweden, and France.

The traditional dances have evolved into a few main styles, each named after their region of origin. Cotswold Morris is what the older generation usually dances, involving handkerchiefs or sticks and outfits of black corduroy knee britches, white stockings, and green sashes. Border Morris (from the English-Welsh border) is a more vigorous style, normally danced with blackened faces while wearing a small strip of bells on the arms or legs. Costumes can be made from ordinary clothes decorated with ribbons or strips of cloth, and the dancers employ sticks. Molly dancing, from East Anglia, is a parody danced in work boots and with at least one man dressed as a woman. The dance itself involves an intricate set of movements in which the dancers weave in and out of each other.

But these old-fashioned Morris styles are in decline, suffering from aging dancers and a lack of new recruits. The dances are seen by the younger generation as eccentric and—especially when waving handkerchiefs—downright silly. Many traditional dancers are concerned that Morris dancing is a dying art that will be extinct in twenty years. Although there are more than 800 Morris sides in England, many are struggling. Yet, they dance on, outside pubs and at festivals every weekend during the summer.

Independent, mixed groups are beginning to supplant the exclusive men-only groups. These younger dancers are quietly transforming the traditional ways to meet modern values. Rivalries emerge as younger men and women reinvent not just the dance but the whole culture around the Morris in startling ways. They incorporate Gothic elements such as black clothes and blackened faces, silver skull rings, and mirrored sunglasses. The women wear purple lipstick, black nail polish, fingerless gloves, and flowing velvet dresses, all atop Doc Martens boots.

Some sides feel that the music and dance recorded in the nineteenth century should be maintained, while others freely

reinterpret the music and dance to suit their abilities and modern influences. They are inventing their own traditions. Some don't use folk tunes at all but write their own music. Their dance style is urban, saucy, and edgy. Fertility dances are decidedly unsubtle. Many performances are timed and themed around Pagan holidays, but some groups pull in ideas of shamanism, ritual theater, and street performance.

While older Morris dancers and enthusiasts don't always accept these modern interpretations and the connection with Pagan rituals as authentic, younger members say the new ways are just as spiritual, and that enacting the Morris dance is just one way to reconnect with the cycle of the year and with the traditions of their country.

In England, groups often meet and practice throughout the winter to hone their dances, then perform them throughout the spring and summer. In the United States, especially in milder climates, groups may perform year round, often gathering for long weekends of dancing or performing at fairs and exhibitions.

Although England has the highest concentration of Morris sides, there are several hundred in North America. To get involved, visit one of the websites at the end of this article to find a local group. There are a multitude of active Morris-related blogs and forums online, and many individual sides have a presence on major social networking sites. Most formal organizations will charge membership dues, whose benefits include access to organized events, magazines and newsletters, and insurance.

And, of course, benefits of Morris dancing are making new friends, getting some exercise, and a chance to reinterpret ancient traditions with a modern twist.

Terminology

Side (or team): a troupe of dancers.

Set: a number of dancers in a particular arrangement for a dance. For example, most Cotswold Morris dances are danced in a rectangular set of six dancers.

Jig: a dance performed by one or two dancers, rather than by a set.

Squire: the leader who speaks for the side in public, leads or calls the dances, and often decides the program for a performance.

Foreman: one who teaches and trains the dancers and is responsible for the style and standard of the side's dancing.

Bagman: the keeper of the bag, the side's funds. In some sides, the bagman acts as secretary and there is a separate treasurer.

Ragman: one who manages and coordinates the team's equipment or costumes.

Fool: usually someone extravagantly dressed who communicates directly with the audience in speech or mime. The fool will often dance around and through the other dancers, without appearing to really be a part of the dance itself.

Beast: a dancer in a costume made to look like a real or mythical animal. Beasts mainly interact with the audience, particularly children. In some groups, this dancer is called the **hobby** (the origin of the "hobby horse").

Ale: a private party with food and beer where a number of Morris sides get together and perform dances for their own enjoyment rather than for an audience. Occasionally an evening ale will be combined with a day or weekend of dance, where all the invited sides will tour the area and perform in public. In North America, the term is used to describe a full weekend of dancing involving public performances and sometimes workshops. The name refers to church- or village-sponsored events where ale or beer was sold to raise funds and Morris dancers were often employed.

RESOURCES

Morris Ring, www.themorrisring.org
The Morris Federation, www.morrisfed.org
Open Morris, www.open-morris.org
Mainly Morris, www.mainlymorrisdancing.org.uk

Chandra Moira Beal *has published hundreds of books and articles. She has been writing for Llewellyn since 1998, and she lives in California with her husband and three house rabbits. Visit www.chandrabeal.com to learn more.*

Illustrator: Rik Olson

Healing Tree Damage

JD Hortwort

In practically any TV show or movie dealing with fantasy topics, the trees we see are gnarled and knotted. The tree's grizzly bark seems to convey great age, possibly wisdom, or maybe sinister motive. We fall into the same pattern in everyday life. Look around any store catering to alternative religions and you will likely find artwork, either photos or drawings, that illustrates trees inhabited by gnomes or fairies who come and go through the bulbous knots and hollowed openings of trees.

This brings to mind Mark Twain's observations in *Life on the Mississippi*. As a young man, Twain fantasized about the Mississippi River. The sunset dancing over the lazy, smooth surface of the water and the ripples of the river's currents drifting over a sandbar, spurring his imagination and fueling his drive to become a riverboat captain. Only after years of training did Twain learn to read those beautiful signs in a different, more practical way. A smooth surface meant deep water and a safe passage. Dainty ripples spelled danger. Twain said after his education he could never look at the river again with the same sense of mystery. He did, however, retain his sense of awe.

The same can be said of trees. In the mundane world, knots and holes on trees aren't fairy openings to the Other World, they are damage to the tree, which could potentially shorten the life of that tree. While not much can be done to fix old damage, people can and should take steps to help trees heal when the damage first occurs. That help can be of a very practical sort, but it can also be spiritual.

Start with a basic understanding of the tree in this world. The outer bark of a tree is dead material, the thickness of which varies depending on the species. The inner bark, just under the outer bark, carries nutrients down to the roots. The cambium layer is next, which is responsible for transporting water up the tree and for the tree's healing process. The cambium layer is also the tree ring. Each year, the tree adds another cambium layer or ring. Again, depending on the tree, between four and twenty layers of cambium are alive. Tallied together, these layers are called the sap wood. The inner most part of the tree is the heart wood. Heart wood is not alive.

With this very basic understanding, it should be easier to see why damage to a tree can be critical. Make a scuff in the dead, outer bark and the result may be unsightly, but it won't be deadly. Break the inner bark and you've disrupted the flow of nutrients to the tree roots. Cut deeper and you've interrupted the movement of water to the top of the tree. Either of the last two breaks can allow invaders into the tree's system.

Damage to trees can come from multiple sources. Construction equipment seems to have an affinity for trees. Some construction sites look almost like a grown-up version of a bumper car attraction at the amusement park! Tree bark can be scuffed or peeled from the trunk as bulldozers careen off them. Homeowners can cause similar damage with mowers or weed trimming equipment.

Then there is the damage that is beyond human control. Winds from strong summer storms, ice from winter storms, extreme temperatures, lightning strikes . . . it's enough to send a tree cowering for cover!

In all of these instances, time is of the essence. The damage must be fixed quickly. Ideally, repairs should be made in the first twenty-four hours after the injury. All is not lost if forty-eight to seventy-two hours have passed but, as with injuries in humans, the quicker you work to fix the problem, the better.

If the bark is broken but not removed from the tree, you can push the bark back in place. Bark that is peeled back from an encounter with a car bumper or a mower can be pulled back to its original location. When the damage occurs on a tree trunk or branch that is less than 2 feet in circumference, duct tape can be used to firmly secure the damaged tissue in place.

The damage must be fixed quickly. Ideally, repairs should be made in the first twenty-four hours after the injury.

When working with large wounds or damage done on tree parts that are greater than 2 feet in diameter, you may have to use galvanized nails to "stitch" the damage back together. Push the damaged bark back into its original location and use the galvanized nails to pin it in place. Obviously, the size of the nail needed will depend on the size of the wound. Just as when a doctor uses a metal pin to help hold a broken bone in place, the nails serve as lynch pins to hold the material in place while the tree heals.

When these types of repairs are done quickly and the damage covers less than 25 percent of the tree trunk, the injury should heal over in time. If you have used duct tape to secure the damage, you may have to replace it a time or two until you see that the healing process is taking hold. At that point, remove the duct tape; nails do not need to be removed.

Larger injuries may never heal over completely. Still, if you have helped the tree partially heal itself, you have improved its chances for a longer life.

Sometimes putting the bark back in place isn't an option—perhaps the bark has been stripped by an animal or a storm has blown it away. In these cases, surgery is the next option. Using a sharp knife, carefully trim the damaged bark away. Go all the way back to clean, healthy inner bark. Try to make rounded cuts. A circle is better than a diamond or an oval with sharp points. Rounded repairs facilitate the movement of nutrients down the trunk and water up the trunk.

Whether you have replaced or removed damaged bark, keep an eye on the wound. It may become necessary to treat the damaged area with an insecticide to keep bugs at bay. We ooze blood when our skin is broken; trees ooze sap. Sugar is a main component of sap, and sugar is a powerful attractant for bugs.

An insecticide is the only thing that should be used on a wounded tree. Tree paints and homemade patches made of roofing tar or cement will interfere with the tree's ability to heal itself. If you have done your job of assisting with a quick repair, that is enough. Have faith and allow Nature to manage the rest.

The next best thing you can do is share some of your energy with the tree in a meditation. Many of us have felt the beautiful, mysterious energy that courses through the plants in our own little world. A meditation under an ancient oak can be a wonderful experience, especially when you work with the tree to travel out into the Universe.

Pick a time when you are calm and well rested. You can't help another entity if you're frazzled yourself. If possible, let this be a time when all other human traffic around the tree is gone (unless you are doing a group meditation for the tree). When doing this practice on property that does not belong to you, such as a public park, make certain you will be safe.

If you have a portable music player, select music that can facilitate your meditation. Bring appropriate stick incense such as rosemary or rose. Both of these scents are powerful healing ingredients.

Begin the music and safely light the incense. Ground and center in the manner of your tradition. If this is your first effort and you have not found a tradition, simply settle yourself under the tree. Breathe deeply, becoming aware of the surroundings. Pull your focus to the tree. Experience the surroundings as you imagine the tree does.

Reach out and touch the tree. If possible, touch the damaged portion. Feel for the energy. If you don't sense the tree's energy, just be aware it is there. All life is energy. Sometimes we sense it in a particular place, sometimes we don't. Nevertheless, it is always there.

Do not try to "feel" the tree's pain. Your focus should be on positive, healing energy. Let your energy flow from your hand to the tree. Let it merge with the tree's energy. See the tree as a complete, healthy entity. It is full of vigor. It is a whole being. Animals thrive in its canopy. People are happy down below. Every day, the tree draws on the cycles of Nature, unfolding under the vibrant sun, challenging the wind, drawing sustenance from the earth, soaking up the rains.

Enjoy this sense of oneness, this bond with the tree, for as long as it feels right. As you begin to pull back to an awareness of yourself as a separate being, give the tree your wish and hope for its full recovery. Come back to yourself.

You can repeat this meditation as many times as it feels necessary. This kind of connection can create a special bond between you and the tree. If you feel welcomed by the tree, you may find it a strong partner in future meditations.

Even if you never connect with the tree again, chances are that as time goes by, you won't walk past it without a smile. Revel in the feeling, your special secret friendship with an enduring entity in Nature.

JD Hortwort *currently resides in North Carolina. She is an avid student of herbology and gardening, a professional writer, and an award-winning journalist.*

Illustrator: Tim Foley

Witchcraft On a Shoestring

Deborah Blake

One of the complaints I hear the most often from other witches is that it costs a lot of money to maintain an active witchcraft practice. Cloaks and garb, athames and wands, crystals, books, candles, herbs, tarot cards, and statuary can all add up to a major drain on your wallet—and that's before you have everyone over for the big Beltane feast!

But it doesn't have to be that way. In fact, I not only believe it is possible to practice the Craft for very little money, I've been doing so for many years. Heck, I even wrote a book about it.

Like this article, it is called *Witchcraft On a Shoestring* (Llewellyn), and it is full of suggestions for how to save money while still having an active and fulfilling witchy life.

Witchcraft on a shoestring isn't just a cute title, though; it is an attitude and an approach to how you practice. What's more, it is simple to learn and easy to apply, regardless of which form of Paganism you follow.

Attitude and Approach

At the heart of witchcraft on a shoestring is one basic realization: all the essentials of a deep and rewarding witchcraft practice are free.

No, really.

If you think about it, what do you really need to be a witch (or Pagan or Wiccan—I'm using the names interchangeably here, since this approach applies to everyone)? You need faith, of course, in whichever god/goddess/gods you worship. A connection to nature and to Earth's ever-changing cycles. And you need the three main tools in every witch's tool chest: Belief, Will, and Focus.

Belief is at the heart of being a Pagan; belief in the gods, belief in yourself and your own place in the universe, and belief in the ability to use magick to create positive change. Will comes from practice and strength of purpose, and focus may be easier when you use tools, but it can certainly be achieved without them. All these things are the core of a witchcraft practice. And they are all free.

Setting Priorities

Of course, just because it is possible to be a well-rounded witch without having any of the aforementioned extras doesn't mean that most of us are going to give up buying tools, wear blue jeans to rituals, and never purchase a book again (goddess forbid!). Witchcraft on a shoestring doesn't call for you to stop spending money. What it does require is that you take a serious look at how you spend your dollars, and what you spend them on. That means setting priorities.

In order to figure out what your priorities are, you first need to take a good look at your own personal magickal practice, as well as your budget, your skills, and how much time you have to devote to creating cheaper alternatives to premade tools.

When examining the ways you perform the Craft, for instance, you may want to take into consideration whether or not you are a solitary or a group witch; how well you are able to concentrate your focus without the aid of tools such as candles, crystals, incense, etc.; how often you practice; and how prominent your witchcraft practice is in your life.

For instance, a solitary witch whose main magickal activity is lighting a candle outside under the full moon and saying a prayer to the goddess will need different items than a witch who runs a large coven and celebrates new moons, full moons, and all eight sabbats in full garb, complete with drumming, formal ritual and spellcasting, and a feast to follow. Each individual's needs will be different, based on how, when, and with whom they practice. So start by figuring out exactly what it is you do, as a witch, and what the minimum requirements are for supporting that activity.

Then take a look at what you have already, and what you still need to purchase. For instance, if you already have three large crystals, you probably don't need another one. That isn't to say you can't buy another one or ten if you love crystals and you have the money to spare, but you might want to save your money for something else more vital.

Another thing to consider is your skill level. Can you sew? If you can, then maybe you can make your own cloak, and save yourself the price (often quite high) of one purchased from a catalog or at a faire. Can you build an altar, carve an athame from wood, or make your own candles? You can save a lot of money making things yourself, if you have the time and the necessary skills. And sometimes you can swap your talents for those you don't have. The members of my coven, Blue Moon Circle, have a wide variety of skill sets, and

we often take turns either creating items for the group or teaching the other members how to do so themselves.

Again, you need to balance the time and energy it takes to make less expensive alternatives at home with the money you will save by doing so. Only you can decide which is in more plentiful supply: money or time.

The reason you set priorities before setting out to practice witchcraft on a shoestring is simple—it is the only way to figure out where you want to put your hard-earned money. But even when you choose what you need to have for your practice, you can look for ways to get these things as cheaply as possible.

Inexpensive Substitutes

Witchcraft is based, in great part, on our own instincts and on general principles of magick. We use tools and correspondences to focus our Will more strongly, for instance, but that doesn't mean we are limited to using specific items, even when they are called for in a spell.

Say, for instance, that you are doing a love spell you found in a book, and the spell calls for a large pink candle, a cup of rose petals, and an amethyst crystal. And let's assume, just for the moment, that you don't happen to have any of those things. Ouch. I can hear your wallet screaming from here.

Instead of running out to the nearest New Age shop to buy all those supplies, let's look at the intention behind each one. All those items are associated with love magick. But there are other ways to use these same tools, without spending a lot of money.

You could use that white candle you already have, and tie a pink ribbon or piece of string around it. If the ribbon is wide enough, you could even write the spell on it. Instead of the cup of rose petals, you could use a single rose (if you grow roses, then it would be free, of course, but even at the store a single rose doesn't cost much), or a few petals left over from the last time you needed one, or even a picture of a rose. And instead of the amethyst crystal, you might use a small tumbled piece (much cheaper), or even a rose quartz crystal, which is also associated with love magick and tends to be much cheaper.

There are many other ways to substitute inexpensive alternatives for more expensive supplies. Here are ten easy suggestions:

- Grow your own herbs. Seeds are cheap, and most herbs will grow in a small space like a windowsill. As a bonus, many of the herbs we commonly use for magick—like parsley, thyme, rosemary, dill, and basil—also have culinary uses. Win, win. (Of course, before consuming any magickal herb, it is a good idea to double-check and make sure it is edible!)

- Make your own garb. If you aren't any good at sewing, you can always "repurpose" funky clothes you find at a consignment store or yard sale. I have lots of vaguely Pagan-looking clothes that I've picked up for a dollar or two. You can also take something simple, like a white shirt, and decorate it with Pagan symbols to turn it into something more witchy.

- Use a pretty plate or bowl instead of a fancy candleholder. Inexpensive glass and pottery often works quite well, as long as it is fire-safe.

- If you want a special chalice for Cakes and Ale but don't want to invest in a pewter or silver one, go to the dollar store and get a glass goblet. You can make it special by tying ribbons around the stem or decorating it using glass markers.

- Instead of a pricey, store-bought athame, take a walk in the woods and find just the right piece of wood. (This works for wands as well.) If it is large enough, you can carve runes or symbols onto it, or you can tie ribbons, leather, crystals, beads, or feathers to it, if you happen to have some lying around. If you don't want to go to even that much trouble, just use your finger to point with. Since the main purpose of an athame is to direct energy, a finger or your hand will work just as well as a physical athame in most circumstances.

- If you need a Book of Shadows, you can use a notebook or a 3-ring binder. Cover it with cloth or fancy paper, or decorate it with Craft symbols. Even better, create a special cover by gluing on leaves and other natural objects.

- You can spend a lot of money on premade spell candles that are anointed with magickal oils, carved with arcane symbols, and consecrated for magickal use. Or you can do all those things yourself and spend the money you save on ingredients to make your own magickal oils—that way you can anoint a whole lot more candles down the line.

- As you can imagine, I'm a big fan of buying books. By all means, feel free to buy the ones I've written! On the other hand, even I don't buy every book I ever want to read. (Almost, but not quite. We talked about priorities, and books are one of mine.) You can get books from the library for free (although it can often be hard to find Pagan books there) or go to one of the many online book swapping sites. One of my coven mates has actually found quite a few Pagan books at yard sales over the years. You can also share books with your Pagan friends, although I wouldn't do that with anything you can't stand to not get back.

- Most of us use votives or tapers for quarter candles. Votives tend to be fairly cheap, and you don't need anything fancier. But if you want to save your money (or can't burn candles wherever you are, be it a hotel room or a dorm room), you can substitute symbols for earth, air, fire, and water—try using a rock, a feather, a picture or drawing of a flame, and a seashell.

- Statues of specific gods and goddesses can be truly beautiful … and truly expensive. If you follow a particular deity, try using something that symbolizes them, like a cat for Bast, or an antler for Herne.

Feeding a Crowd

When you are a Solitary witch, you can easily control what you do and don't spend money on. But when you practice with others, things can be a little trickier.

A perfect example of this is the post-ritual feast. I have been to—and in my earlier days as a high priestess, hosted—any number of rituals where the person hosting the event cooked up a huge feast single-handedly. If you're someone who likes to cook for your friends, this can be a lot of fun. It can also be a tremendous amount of work and darned expensive. If you have a large coven, or hold open rituals that might draw twenty or thirty people or more, it can easily break the monthly food budget.

A better choice is to have your feasts be "pot luck." Everyone who will be attending is instructed to bring a dish to pass. If you are really organized, or are in a smaller group like a Blue Moon Circle, it can be a good idea to check ahead of time to see what people are bringing; that way you don't end up with three loaves of bread and no vegetables.

A better choice is to have your feasts be "pot luck." Everyone who will be attending is instructed to bring a dish to pass.

There have been times in the past when there were circle members who we knew had little or no extra money. These folks were usually given the most inexpensive options: potatoes, rice, or pasta, for instance. My book has an entire section devoted to recipes that will feed a crowd for under ten dollars, and almost all of them are dishes we have made and enjoyed.

Some items, like the potatoes and pasta above, are almost always pretty cheap. But you can also save money by planning your feast around seasonal foods (a good Pagan tradition anyway), since produce that is in season is usually considerably cheaper than that which isn't. Asparagus, for instance, is a pricey treat most of the year—except in spring, when it is readily available. Buying locally grown food can often save you money, too, especially if you have a farmers' market near you. And you're supporting local farmers, which I'm sure the Goddess thinks is a good idea.

Of course, if you have a garden, using fruits and vegetables you have grown yourself is not only a cheaper option, but it has the added benefit of sharing all that energy you put into the process. And it connects you down through the past with all the Pagans of yore who grew and harvested their own food.

Let's not forget to look for sales, either. You might have planned to serve chicken, for example, but if the ground beef is on a buy one pound, get one free sale, you may just want to change the menu. It pays to be flexible, as well as frugal.

Nature Is Free

When trying to keep down the costs of your Pagan practice, remember that witchcraft is a nature-based religion, and therefore much of what is involved needn't cost anything at all.

For instance, you can take a walk in the woods and connect with the trees and the creatures that live in them. Even a park in the city

can have a few spots that might allow you to get back to your roots (so to speak). Sit by the water—ocean, lake, stream—it doesn't matter how big or small. Just take a few moments to listen to the sound of the water and let it soothe you. And think about how all the water on the planet is connected, and through it, you are connected, too. Go outside at night and look at the stars. Feel how small you are, and yet, how much a part of the whole of the universe. Gaze at the moon when it is full, and talk to the Lady whose symbol it is.

. . . .

This is just the tip of the iceberg. There are hundreds of ways to practice witchcraft for little or no money. After all, being a witch isn't really about how many crystals you have or who has the fanciest athame. At its core, witchcraft is a path of heart and mind, of love and faith. And that, my friends, doesn't cost a thing.

Deborah Blake *is the author of* Circle, Coven and Grove: A Year of Magickal Practice, Everyday Witch A to Z , The Goddess is in the Details, Everyday Witch A to Z Spellbook, *and* Witchcraft On a Shoestring, *all from Llewellyn. She has published numerous articles in Pagan publications, including Llewellyn annuals and has an ongoing column in* Witches & Pagans Magazine. *Her award-winning short story,* "Dead and (Mostly) Gone" *is included in the* Pagan Anthology of Short Fiction *(Llewellyn, 2008). Deborah has been interviewed on television, radio, and podcast, and can be found online at Facebook, Twitter, and www .myspace.com/deborahblakehps. When not writing, Deborah runs* The Artisans' Guild, *a cooperative shop she founded with a friend in 1999, and also works as a jewelry maker. She lives in a 100-year-old farmhouse in rural upstate New York with five cats who supervise all her activities, both magickal and mundane.*

Illustrator: Bri Hermanson

Needles, Threads, and Pins

Gail Wood

There's nothing more ordinary than sewing on a button or replacing something lost, torn, or falling off. It's a chore. Mending things is something every household has to do, even if there is no interest in sewing or the needle arts. For the most part, our mending piles up until it demands our attention, and then it's an arduous mess to clean up. We grumble and complain as we sew on buttons, mend tears, and take up hems.

What if we were to shift our attitude and make the ordinary act of mending a magical spell? After all, the meaning

Needles, safety pins,
and thread

Buttons, scissors,
and those snaps.

Magic and love
here embed

In mending, sewing,
household tasks.

of the word *mundane* also means being of the earth, or of worldly matters. The word came to be about ordinary events because mundane matters were not the concerns of heaven. As Pagans and Wiccans, we know that the matters of the earth may well be ordinary, but those are also matters of sacred and divine life. Everything we do is sacred and our every action is that of a divine being—even mending and sewing! Much of our magical work concerning the soul and the heart uses the word *mending*. It's a wonderful analogy for healing our fractured lives. If we move from the analogy back to the source, we arrive at our pile of mending and sewing.

Sewing and mending magic (like all household magic) is short, simple, and practical. In order to finish the household tasks of cooking, cleaning, and repairing, the magic needs to be quick, practical, and effective. Banish the thoughts of creating big rituals and ceremonies and move your mind to simple charms and tiny ritual reminders. The beginning of all good work—especially good magical work—starts with the tools, and it is the same for mending and sewing. How do you store and treat your mending tools? Are they all in one place? Are they blessed and consecrated? Do you honor and treat them as you would your tools for magical and spellwork?

A basic household mending kit is very simple. Most of what you'll need to do is repair work, so you need a variety packet of needles, safety pins, a measuring tape or ruler, scissors, thread, an assortment of buttons, and perhaps some iron-on patches. If you darn socks, you will need darning tools as well. I keep my mending tools in a sewing box I got at a chain fabric and craft store. It's smallish and had stayed on the store's sale shelf for a long time because it was damaged. As the price decreased, my usually-absent nerve increased; I finally bargained with the manager to get the box for nearly free!

Because I do a lot of sewing and crafts, I have other tool boxes that are outfitted more fully for knitting or quilting, but this is the one I take when we travel to various events and might need something repaired or need an impromptu magical spell. Your own sewing repair box may vary. I have a couple of different sizes of scissors (well maintained and sharp), a variety packet of needles, straight pins, safety pins, measuring tape, some buttons in different colors, and threads in the colors of white, brown, black, red, and navy blue. I sometimes add in tape, glue, and paper scissors as well. I also put in a small egg rattle to remind me that this is one of my magical tool kits; I use the rattle for cleansing and centering before beginning my task.

After cleaning, repairing, and filling my box, I set it on my altar for a moon phase, allowing it time to experience some magical workings and the full cycle of the moon. At the new moon, I blessed it before the gods and the elements with this enchantment:

> Spinner Clotho spin the thread,
> Lachesis the apportioner, measure the charge,
> Atropos the inevitable, cut the measure,
> Please bless these tools to their task
> For mending, sewing, all sorts of repair.
> Imbue their work with love, joy, and magic,
> Conscious and Unconscious
> The magic does mend.
> Reverence and mirth,
> Power and joy,
> Honor and humility
> Each stitch does employ.
> This magic and power
> Through my hands and my tools

Repairs and mends the heart and soul.
With your blessings,
For the good of all
And the harm of none.
As I will it so mote it be!

After raising a cone of power and grounding the energy in the sewing box, I put it in its place to do its work.

There are many household goddesses and goddesses of creativity and needlecrafts in every culture of the world. Athena is the goddess with whom I work most frequently for this and other areas; however, as I pondered who to work with for this tool kit, the Moirae stepped in to take the foreground. These three Fates of the Greek guided the life stories of humans, and even the gods could not influence them. Clotho was the spinner who spun the thread of our lives, Lachesis decided the length of each person's life, and Atropos made the final cut, the snip that ended life and began the journey to the land of the dead. So to them I committed my tools of repair and mending.

And yet the Moirae are not the only deities I work with for mending and sewing. Hestia, Vesta, Brigit, Xochiquetzal, Ix Chel, Athena, Arachne, Erinia, Spider Woman, and First Woman are all well known goddesses of the hearth or of the needle arts. It isn't always easy to identify gods and goddesses associated with the needle arts. As a so-called womanly art, needlework and sewing is a humbler craft than some of the larger issues such as war, fertility, nature, etc.; many of the needle goddesses' attributes are lost in time. So as we research the gods, we need to be well aware that our own personal interaction and understanding of the gods is as reliable and authentic as the documented historical evidence. If you are called

to consecrate your needlework to Aphrodite, heed her call! Choose your goddess wisely but remember the gods ultimately choose us.

Each tool in your mending kit can be charmed to bless its work. Sometimes in the middle of the hurly burly of getting things done, it's hard to remember to stop and do the magic and then solve the problem. Recognizing that each of our mundane tools has a magical purpose and enchanting them at the beginning of the task can ensure that magic is imbued in the foundations of our mending. Our tools are ready always to be both magical and practical.

Scissors

Scissors are a wonderful tool, as they are sharp and shiny. I am picky about scissors, so I buy a particular brand. There are scissors to cut paper and others to cut fabric (be sure to buy the right ones for your needs); large ones for big jobs and small ones for projects that challenge us to use our fine motor skills. Still other cutting tools are made for snipping threads and getting close into the work. In my mending kit, I have a pair of scissors in the shape of a heron, a bird sacred to me, which is almost always used for ritual items. I have embroidery scissors, paper scissors, and two sizes of fabric scissors. Naturally all you really need for mending is a large pair and a small pair. Keep them sharp and free of the fuzz that develops from cutting thread and fabric. Scissors have an esoteric history as well, as in the story of Atropos. A sharp, clean pair of scissors honors the work, no matter how hard or how difficult. A charm for scissors is:

> *Scissors, scissors, shiny and bright*
> *Make my cuts straight and right.*
> *Ragged edges made clean and new*
> *Shows my magic, loving and true.*

Spoken three times with the scissors in your hand, your scissors become empowered with the energy of love to do their job with skill and magic.

NEEDLES

Needles with their eyes for thread bespeak of the ability to connect and bring things together. Of course, eyes are seen as a tool of vision, both inner and outer. Running a thread through the eye and then sewing something together or decorating with thread, the eye is essential for keeping all the tools and materials together and for creating the vision of the project.

Needles bend with long use, and their outer polish is rubbed off. Their sharp point wears down. It's important to replace your needles periodically. The Japanese have the Festival of Broken Needles,

Hari-kauyo, where all the old needles are gathered together and brought to Buddhist and Shinto temples. The old needles are then placed in cakes of tofu. The idea is that the sorrows and joys of the women sewing are passed through the needle. This festival, on February 8, honors the service of the needles and the spirit of small, practical tools. I replace my needles on a regular basis, retiring them to a witch's bottle, something I make as a housewarming gift for my friends in the Craft. My charm for old needles is:

> Though my shiny needle grows dull,
> Magic and love never lulls.
> With magic and thanks you retire
> Into the rest you aspire.

Thankfully, the gods are amused by rhymes and charms, and it doesn't always take high literary art to enchant and thank your tools. A charm for new needles can be light and fun:

> To my bright and shiny needle
> Hear me call, hear me wheedle!
> Keep my stitches straight and true,
> Magic and love sewn through and through.

BUTTONS

Buttons are fascinating, and whole books have been written about their history and art. Today buttons are a mass-produced, easily obtained everyday object. But they also go beyond ordinary: people collect them and there's a collector's market for unusual buttons. In ancient times, buttons were a precious commodity used in trade. They were used sparingly because they were rare. Women passed down their button boxes to their daughters, nieces, and female relations. I've inherited a few button boxes—one came when my mother, a sewer, gave me a gallon jar of buttons my grandmother (a quilter, knitter, and sewer) had gotten from the old shirt factories in town. There must be thousands of buttons in that jar. I've given a quart of them to a local charity that teaches people the sewing arts and works with the local disability charities to teach people working skills. I've also shared them with friends and my witch sisters.

Buttons are an art and a craft, but they are also very utilitarian. They fasten things together. They keep our clothes from revealing our private secrets. They keep us neat and orderly, and they are often found on our body, even next to our skin. Thus they can absorb our secrets, our hopes, and our fears.

Buttons come in various colors, patterns, sizes, and shapes; there are even different ways of attaching buttons to fabrics, from holes to shanks. They can serve, in a pinch or by design, as a magical substitute for coins, stones, and other objects. They are practical, portable, and very magical. And these wonderful little objects keep you whole and holy as you go about your daily life. You can charm the buttons already on your clothes, the ones ready to replace lost ones, and the ones you are about to sew on:

White ones, black ones, all the colors,
Buttons keep me in working order.
Magic go round with shanks or holes,
These little buttons keep me whole.

Button Sewing Charms

The thing about mending is that most of it doesn't take long, but each one is individual and requires several steps. Even something as simple as sewing on a button can involve finding a matching button in size and shape, matching the color of the thread, and then measuring to ensure accurate fitting. In sewing on a button, some

magic-based choices can be made. Does the button have two holes are four? Two holes can symbolize partnership and joining together, while four symbolizes the four elements and the solidity of the earth. A two-hole button charm for protection and strength is:

Back and forth, back and forth
With strength and power and with force
To withstand the bad things life can bring
Through my needle, magic sings.
For safety and strength
As I will it so mote it be.

With a four-hole button, you can choose to sew the button on in an X pattern or straight across. You can change the qualities you want to bring into the charm as well. Sewing with an X can "mark the spot," create a spotlight, or designate a space for attention. It can also be a barrier and cancel out negativity. The crossing of two lines can bring together to opposite ideas into one space. It's your choice how you regard the X, and then you can create a charm to make an effect. For a four-hole button, this charm can be used, saying it in pairs. This charm speaks to the opposite ideas in one space.

> *From right to left, from left to right,*
> *Join together in the heart.*
> *Bring together the dark and the light,*
> *Union and harmony to me impart.*

Thread

Thread is a marvelous thing. Spun from fleece, flax, and other materials, it is placed on long spools. As Clothos reminds us, threads can be long, they can be short, and they can be abruptly cut short. Thread comes in a variety of materials and lasts a very long time. Those made from natural materials do deteriorate over time, but they still last years. Thread colors can help coordinate not only to the project but also to magical intention. Thread connects and binds things together and helps create the intended shape of the garment or other object. To charm your thread:

> *All the colors of my threads,*
> *Magic repairs all tears and shreds.*
> *Sew together with love and care,*
> *Magic my threads for repair.*

Pins

Pins and safety pins are shaped differently but do the same thing in different levels of permanence and safety. They hold things together while we are waiting for a more lasting solution. Straight pins are long and sharp and sometimes their heads come in different colors. They hold things together but often fall out and can prick people. They are intended for the short-term use, while safety pins with their ability to hide their point can hold two items together for longer. Sometimes safety pins become the permanent solution to damage just because we forget or put off fixing them. Removing pins during mending often signals the end of a tear and the beginning of the renewed object. To charm your pins:

Long and straight, bless my pins,
As my magical work begins.
Bent and safe, bless my pins,
As my magical work begins.
Hold things together firm and right,
Bless my sewing day and night.

Measuring Tools

Measuring tapes and rulers are very helpful in mending and sewing. You probably need both. The tape is for larger projects, and its flexibility allows you to measure the body and body parts. A six-inch ruler helps with the placement of buttons and other items. These items can symbolically take the measure of the person and the project, a reminder of Lachesis apportioning out the time of our lives. A way to bless your measuring tools is this charm:

Bless this tool of measure,
May it reveal magical treasure.
Length and breadth of magic and love,
As below, so from above.

. . . .

There are also other tools, such as snaps, iron-on patches, and darning tools. You will soon come to know what you need most. It's simple to write the little charms: write four lines with the same rhythm, use a rhyming pattern, and then practice it a little bit. If it resonates with you and makes you smile, then you've got a charm to make the gods smile and bless your tools!

Now that your tools are charmed and ready, you can tackle your mending with the knowledge that your work will be imbued with love and magic. If you wish to add magical energy to your mending, you can do that to the entire pile of mending or to each project as you begin.

> Here is my mending in a pile,
> Magic makes it worth my while.
> To sew, patch, and repair,
> To will, to know, and finish as I dare!
> For the finish with the harm of none,
> And the good of all, so mote it be.

You have focused your will and magic to accomplish your mending. If you wish to further empower it, you can include a time or deadline in the rhyme.

With good intentions, funny little charms, and empowered tools, you can move your earthly mundane chores into the realm of the sacred. The ordinary becomes extraordinary in the hands of the skilled and capable witch.

Gail Wood's *bio appears on page 112.*

Illustrator: Kathleen Edwards

Shopping for the Magickal Amid the Mundane

Blake Octavian Blair

If you're lucky enough to live within a reasonable distance of a metaphysical, New Age, or occult shop, you may not give a second thought as to where you can obtain your witchy supplies. However, I often find myself in conversation with those not lucky enough to be near such a store, and they express frustration and exasperation about where they are ever going to find that much-sought-after ritual supply or spell ingredient. In this day and age, of course, there are a myriad of websites and online shops; however, it is also a good idea to try balancing Internet resources with supporting your community's economy by shopping locally. In reality, the answer to your magickal needs may be closer than you think.

Many commonly desired magickal supplies can be found on shelves among seemingly mundane merchandise. A good place to start is your local grocery store. Yes, the one you visit regularly for your milk and bread. Grocery stores often carry treasures that are overlooked by even the most frequent customer. Most grocery stores have at least a moderately decent selection of herbs and spices in the cooking aisle. The rosemary you need for that protection spell or the eucalyptus you need for healing work could well be waiting for you in aisle 5 next to the flour and sugar. While you're there, let's not forget to pick up a witch's staple: sea salt.

Many commonly desired magickal supplies can be found on shelves among seemingly mundane merchandise.

You might be lucky to live in an area with a particularly high multicultural population. The area I live in has a fairly large Hispanic population and the local grocery store carries a plethora of bulk spices imported from Mexico, as well as a large variety of inexpensive seven-day novena candles, both plain and with various deity and religious images. This find is considered a great score for candle magick workers as well as for those who might practice or incorporate Vodou, Hoodoo, or Santería into their path. Novena candles are perfect for long-term and ongoing spellwork. You may be thinking to yourself, "What about those everyday 'on the fly' spells?" A quick and easy solution is to head to the baking aisle and pick up a pack of birthday candles. They have a short burn time and come in a variety of colors, fitting the bill nicely.

This brings us to another prime place to check for magickal supplies: ethnic grocers. Asian grocery stores often carry a selection of Feng Shui supplies as well as statuary and trinkets such as money frogs, Maneki Nekos (lucky cats), and Hotei Buddha figurines. Who couldn't use a little extra prosperous energy and a little bit of Feng Shui to bring things into harmony? Of course, while you're there, don't forget to look for those amazing tea sets they often carry as well as the great selection of affordable herbal teas. I'm lucky enough to also live only about half an hour from a "Little India." There is a wonderful Indian grocery there that carries not only delectable edibles but also an array of Hindu puja (ritual) supplies.

Kum kum powder, offering trays and bowls, incense burners, deity murtis (statues), discounted bulk incense, and more can be found here—a delight for those incorporating Asian traditions. It's only a matter of looking in the right places and keeping your options open.

There is yet another place you should keep your magickal eyes open while you are grocery shopping: your local farmers' market. These markets often have a wide selection of seasonal fruits and vegetables to be included in tasty kitchen witch creations, as well as potted herbs that you can plant in your garden. Farmers' markets and peoples' markets are also stocked with local arts and crafts; you might just find the perfect chalice from a local potter, or come across locally spun yarn for crocheting a magickal creation.

This would also support independent entrepreneurs and your local economy.

Don't forget to add a trip to the dollar store to your magickal shopping rounds. This can be an excellent place not only for candles, holders, small knick-knacks of animal totems, and other things magickally symbolic, but also for sabbat decorations. I have more than once found wonderful altar decorations and components at the dollar store. They always have a plethora of new seasonal merchandise as the wheel of the year turns. Dollar stores also have proven to be a good source for various candles. Especially good finds include black candles near Samhain and gold and silver candles, which are generally carried closer to the winter holidays.

If you're feeling a bit adventurous, a great place to consider spending an interesting morning or even the better part of a day is a flea market. Flea markets can be feast or famine, but you'll almost always find something worth your trip if you keep a keen eye. Old glass milk bottles, horseshoes, cauldrons, antique and foreign coins, stray keys (both antique and contemporary), cast iron trivets with magickal knotworks, and even pentacles can be found. Hunting for bargain-priced used occult books is also a more common occurrence than one might think. You may also find inexpensive old apothecary jars to store your herbs in, as well as flats of canning jars priced at next to nothing—a kitchen witch's goldmine! Flea markets are actually a great place to keep your eyes peeled for bona fide occult and Pagan booths. More than once, when you'd least expect it, I've rounded a corner or stumbled into a nook and found myself in a small closet-sized botanica or a corner booth run by Pagans brimming with herbs, books, candles, tarot decks, and a selection of jewelry. Flea markets are becoming popular venues for occult and Pagan vendors because the overhead cost for the space is much lower than more permanent types of retail space. In some cases, this results not only in a larger profit margin for the shopkeeper but also lower prices for the customer.

Continue your local shopping adventure at antique and thrift stores. When it comes to antique shops, prices can vary widely from great bargains to high bounties aimed at wealthy collectors, but they are always worth a look. Old coffee tables and dressers can have new life breathed into them when reincarnated as altar tables or herbal apothecary cabinets. Keep your eye out for these finds at the local thrift stores. I actually found a lovely small handmade tile mosaic table for just six dollars at a thrift store run by the local school district's PTA. It now serves as a goddess altar that we decorate with appropriate foliage each season.

It is also important to note that many thrift stores are run by charitable organizations as fundraisers for their causes. Shopping

at these businesses can be a form of giving back to your community. As magickal practitioners, we often discuss how the energy you put out into the universe will return to you. This is obviously true for our magickal workings but it's also important to realize that it is true outside of our rituals and spellwork. Giving back to your community is something that will return to you in a beneficial manner, both physically and metaphysically. These transactions create a truly win/win situation.

There is an old and well-worn pun that "witches are Crafty people." This phrase endures because of its truth! Most Pagans have a talent and/or skill in some type of art or craft. We are all well aware of the fact that any magickal tool or item you put your time, effort, and energy into making will be far more powerful than anything purchased in the store. This brings us to your local arts and crafts shop. Walk the aisles and soak in the inspiration: beads to craft into magickal jewelry; wood to paint, carve, or burn into protective charms and talismans; clay to be sculpted into runes; wooden boxes waiting to be finished, stained, painted, or decoupaged into spell and tarot boxes; yarn to be knitted into a ritual shawl ... the list goes on and on.

Akin to the craft store is another much-overlooked source: hardware and home improvement stores. Do you have an affinity for power tools or working with your hands? Were you unable to find that perfect altar table or herb cabinet at the thrift store or flea market? No problem. Draw up some plans, head to the local home improvement store, and pick up some lumber, stain, and other supplies. Soon you'll be on the way to building yourself custom magickal furniture! Another option to consider if carpentry isn't one of your stronger skills is the purchase of a ready-made wall shelf. Home improvement stores carry a wide selection of such shelves these days. A wall-mounted shelf serves as a great shrine or altar if you are living in a small space or have children or pets you are worried about getting into your ritual items. Or perhaps you have an existing magickal cupboard or old dresser you use as an altar and it's looking a bit tired. One great way to spruce up such furnishings is to pick out new drawer knobs or pulls. These can totally change the character of a piece, turning it from dreary to dazzling. Home improvement stores often carry fun novelty pulls, such as leaves or Celtic knots, or ones made of glass or metals.

For those who do much magickal work with plants and herbs, one option always up for consideration is growing your own plants and herbs in a magickal garden.

A perfect shopping stop for the green witch is the local plant nursery. You will likely find almost any plant you're looking for, as well as some you probably didn't even know existed. They'll stock houseplants, garden plants, annuals, perennials, a selection of herbs, and even seeds if you prefer to start from the ground up, literally. You can't beat the expertise of nursery employees. Oftentimes, employees at locally owned nurseries are knowledgeable especially as to what will grow in your region and under what conditions. If you live in an apartment or have little to no actual space to plant a garden, never underestimate the power of a container garden on a porch, patio, or windowsill. Don't forget to look for both gardening tools and creative pots and containers at the other stops along your magickal shopping route.

Another place to hunt for magickal supplies is the great outdoors. In a busy modern life full of computers, mass transit, and hustle and bustle, this may be easy to overlook. Mother Nature provides us with all the magickal trees, plants, and objects we could desire. Take a walk or hike through local woods, parks, or other areas. You may find a fallen branch that's perfect for a staff or wand. Perhaps you'll catch a leaf falling from an oak tree, which is said to bring good luck. Or maybe you'll happen upon a rock or stone that calls to you for use in magickal work. Just be sure that it is permissible for you to remove the objects from the area in which you are hiking; many nature refuges, preserves, and sanctuaries have rules regarding this.

. . . .

I should, of course, give an obligatory mention that any magickal supplies or tools, whether handcrafted or purchased (especially if they are second hand) should be cleansed and consecrated to remove any energies from previous owners or contact from previous shoppers. After all, you're probably not the only one who admired that beautiful goblet you bought from the flea market to use as a chalice. Give it a quick rinse in salt water, pass it through sage smoke, or leave it in the windowsill in the moonlight.

I always recommend trying to support your local Pagan and metaphysical vendors. If you are not lucky enough to have one nearby, don't fret; magick is still all around you. You simply have to engage your creative muse and explore the abundant existing resources in your area. You'll do fine—Pagans have a wonderful reputation for seeing the magickal amid the mundane.

Blake Octavian Blair's *bio appears on page 122.*

Illustrator: Christa Marquez

Rituals for Open Circles

Ann Moura

What makes a public ritual workable for the experienced witch as well as for the newcomer to Wicca, or even for the merely curious? Having attended numerous open circle rituals for Esbats and Sabbats and having facilitated many in conjunction with spiritual groups, Pagan gatherings, and metaphysical shops including my own, I have gained some important insights from observation and participation. These experiences have taught me to address the comfort level of the attendees and ensure that everyone understands what is going on and what is expected of them during the ritual. As I proceed through a ritual, I provide a basic explanation of what that ritual is about and what I am doing so everyone in the circle grasps the significance of the ritual and how it relates to them personally. Most important, the attendees are able to keep up with the actions taking place and are brought into an active participating role rather than standing silently as observers. I consider open circle rituals of any kind to be a golden opportunity for education tied together with spiritual communion and community bonding.

Comfort and Setting

An open ritual begins with planning and setup, which includes location. If you don't have a large enough indoor space for your ritual, you may consider outdoor spaces. For large groups, renting park or campsite space is another expense to be considered, but generally the guests are charged an attendance fee in these cases.

The length of the ritual is another factor to consider. If outside in the sun or in the black of night, think about how the weather will affect the group and the ritual. Also remember to account for changing weather if your ritual is particularly long; if your ritual begins at sundown on a fall day, temperatures will drop quickly as the sunlight fades.

With small groups outside, the ritual area can be prepared with a canopy for shade if tree shade is not sufficient. If you are outdoors at night, you have the additional problems of people stumbling or falling in the rough terrain, insect control (or lack thereof), lighting for the ritual so people can see what is happening, and sound amplification to allow people to hear over the crickets and frogs. With so many factors involved, taking on the responsibility for outdoor rituals involving hundreds of people is not for the faint of heart and requires many helpers.

Another matter to consider with public outdoor rituals is the reaction of passersby, which should be kept to a minimum so as not to interrupt the ritual. Unless working in a secluded area, I find that taking a less formal approach allows me to breeze through a ritual without any fuss from neighbors or people walking by. Be considerate

of the comfort level of the people at the ritual, especially in regard to public places. Indoor rituals are a good way to avoid that concern, but if the indoor space is too small to accommodate the number of guests, go outside with a confidence that will reassure your guests. For outdoor rituals, I have an altar set up and include customary activities such as jumping the cauldron of burning woods or herbs, but I keep the attire basic and simple. Keep the ritual spiritual, using drumming or music only if it is appropriate and unlikely to be a nuisance to the neighbors. My rituals last no more than half an hour to a maximum of forty-five minutes in order to keep the energy flowing to a strong and satisfying conclusion.

Another variable for public ritual involves standing, sitting, or a combination of both in the circle. Some gatherings attract hundreds of people, so participants are allowed to bring their camp chairs into the circle to accommodate age, health, and fatigue while waiting for everyone to be smudged and enter the space. During this time, it is important to tell people to move deosil/clockwise around the circle and to keep them moving. You can prompt people along, or have helpers (usually stationed at the quarters) to keep the crowd moving until the circle is filled without glaring gaps. Some folks want to be the first in line to enter the circle, but also want to set up their camp chairs early, thus creating a barrier that the other guests have to stumble around. There are always those who do not have a clue about circle courtesy or proper behavior, so a gentle reminder to keep moving or a nudge to step out of the way of traffic may be necessary to keep the crowd in motion and avoid lost tempers. With small groups, standing seems to work well, with a couple of chairs available for those who need them.

ATTIRE

I consider ritual attire to be optional in an open circle, as this allows those who have robes and want to wear them to do so without excluding people who choose to attend in street clothes. The point of having open rituals is to utilize the energy of the lunar phase or Sabbat season in a way that is comfortable for all involved. As the presenter, you should wear something that distinguishes you for that role. It can be ritual wear, a special cloak or decorative duster that feels appropriate, ritual jewelry, or simply your cingulum (knotted belt). It is not the embellishments of jewelry, flowing robes, and crowns of antlers that make a ritual—it is the content and the heart that goes into it that matters.

Getting Started

There are variables in rituals that allow for the facilitator's personal touches to be added in even the rudimentary stages of circle casting, such as sweeping, smudging, bringing in the attendees, and calling the quarters. Alternative methods can be applied with sweeping the circle space, for example. As a ritual tool rather than a cleaning tool, the besom is used to clear the prospective sacred space by moving aside energies that might be counterproductive to the ritual.

From the perspective of moving energy, I usually sweep prior to the guests entering the circle in order to avoid brushing the negative or chaotic energy onto the feet of the guests. The exception to this order of events is when I do a group cleansing. People are then brought into the ritual area and I guide them in drawing together the stressful, negative, or chaotic energies that have upset them or that they sense as barriers to their happiness or fulfillment. These negative energies are gathered starting at the head, pulled together through the body, and pushed down to their feet and cast out as a ball on the floor/ground in front of them. I then take the besom around the circle and carefully gather all the discarded energies and brush these out of the circle for Nature to reclaim, cleanse, and recycle. By explaining my actions throughout the process, everyone knows what is happening, and the magical act is enforced with the power of words.

By explaining my actions throughout the process, everyone knows what is happening, and the magical act is enforced with the power of words.

Smudging the circle after this allows for the attendees to feel the total sensation of cleansing and revitalization. Imbolc is an especially good time for smudging, as the ritual includes purifying and blessing the besom, but I include this group cleansing whenever I feel the collective energy of the guests needs more than smudging with sage.

I usually bring the guests into the sacred space area prior to casting the circle so they can feel the energy of inclusion and can participate in calling the quarters. I have attended rituals where everyone stands around while a group completely sets up the circle, then creates a doorway for the guests to enter, being smudged as they cross the threshold, and I sometimes use this method for Esbats. The threshold can be envisioned or symbolized with a crossed besom and sword, but if using tools, be sure to remind people to step over these objects, as someone inevitably will stumble on them otherwise.

Participation

At the start of an open ritual, I have a volunteer hold the text and turn pages on my signal. In a coven or family setting, this role may be given to a young member of the group, who is called the maiden or the lad. As the presenter, you can do all the parts as though in a Solitary ritual, which provides people with an idea of how they can conduct their own private rituals. If you have others who are able to help out with the ritual, they can take on some of the lines and actions such as smudging, calling the quarters, alternating the spoken portions, helping with blessing the Simple Feast, or distributing food and drink.

Throughout the ritual, giving people clues on what to do helps them feel involved. Let them know when to face the directions and raise their arms to greet or bid farewell to the elementals. Pause a moment for people to repeat aloud certain phrases from the ritual such as "Hail and Welcome," "Hail and Farewell," "Blessed Be," "So Mote It Be," and be ready to prompt with a gesture so they all chime in with "Merry Meet, Merry Part, and Merry Meet Again" at the conclusion of the ritual.

Since Esbats are also a time for magical workings, any kind of activity that draws in the power of the lunar phase can be used in an open circle, but be considerate of the guests. While I have let people select a rune and provided handouts with the meanings, I have also used meditations and opened gateways with a black mirror. Not everyone will participate, and that is fine. The presenter at an Esbat needs to keep an eye on the people in the circle to gauge their comfort level and help them stay at ease. Sometimes the simplest activities are the best, such as sprinkling the guests with blessed lunar water, but this is also a good time for making projects that can be taken home, such as charm bags, talismans, herbal blends, bath salts, and so forth. I have made dozens of small charm bags with herbs and little stones to honor the Faeries at Midsummer, handed out stalks of wheat at Lughnassadh, blessed tea lights for jack o'lanterns at Samhain, and blessed blue chime candles at Imbolc for people to light in their homes. All of these tokens have been well received.

The in-circle activities of meditation, journeying, and divination require a watchful eye to ensure everyone has a positive experience. Most important of all, remember to release any entities called, bid farewell to the deity invoked, and close any doors that have been opened.

A variety of traditions, solitary practices, and newcomers to the Craft can be accommodated in ritual with a generic script. The deities can be named or simply called the Goddess and the God or the Lady and the Lord. I vary the deity names to correspond to the season, such as with Maia and the Greenman at Beltane and the Crone and the Hunter at Samhain. With covens and family or solitary practice, the deities addressed may always be the same ones, but by using different names and representations in open circles, the attendees are able to see a variety of aspects of the Divine.

The script for Sabbats and Esbats should vary sufficiently for regular guests to distinguish what it is that makes one ritual different from another. Be flexible and work with the season or lunar phase, thinking about the significance of each ritual and how best to bring that across to a group that may include newcomers with rudimentary knowledge. I try to incorporate the meanings of my actions as much as possible, and even take into the account the impact of the lunar phase during a Sabbat.

Cakes and Ale

During the Simple Feast (Cakes and Ale/Wine) part of the ritual, I include a blessing of a basket of food and pitcher of beverage to be passed around to the participants. If outdoors, the libation goes directly onto the ground in front of the altar table; if indoors, a libation bowl serves this purpose, and it is later emptied onto the ground outside. It only makes sense to exclude alcoholic beverages when working with a diverse group. There is no way of knowing who is a recovering alcoholic or who has allergies, and alcohol is not suitable for children or pregnant women, so I feel that even having wine as an option is not in the best interests of all the attendees. I stick with antioxidant beverages such as blueberry or cranberry juice, and there are so many cranberry blends that one can be selected to fit the ritual—apple for Mabon, blackberry for Lughnassadh, white cranberry grape for Imbolc, and so on.

The other part of the feast is the food, and again there are allergies and food restrictions to consider. I always tell people the ingredients of food items—such as nuts, seeds, wheat, egg, raisins, gluten, and so on. Still, I will tell participants that if they cannot eat the food, they can take it home for a personal altar or shrine, use it as an offering, or add it to a protective, seasonal charm bag.

The easiest way to handle distribution of the feast is to give a stack of little paper cups to people at different points in the circle and let them take their own and pass the rest. Take back the remaining clean cups and collect the used ones after the feast by restacking and setting aside. Passing a basket with cookies or cut up bread or cake will go quickly. You can let people pass the basket or take it around the circle yourself. I like to take the beverage around in a

pitcher and pour a small amount in each cup—the point of the feast is ritual, not a meal. If there is leftover food or drink, I let people have seconds or take any extra bread home. Most people will start to pass along the stacked used cups, but you can also ask them to do so if you are ready to move on in the ritual. It is easy to discretely set the used cups on the floor/ground by the altar until the ritual is ended and cleanup begins.

Announcements can be made during the ritual meal, letting people know when and where the next ritual will take place, or what activities and events are coming up that relate to the community. This is also a good time to indicate where a container for donations is located so they can help defray the expense of the ritual. Some of the costs involved may include beverages, bread, cups, flowers, altar decorations, candles, incense, handouts such as song sheets, and a token of the ritual for people to take with them for their homes.

If a buffet follows the ritual, people should be notified ahead of time by way of flyers, website postings, etc., that they need to bring something to share. The presenter still needs to ensure there is some food and beverage available, along with plates, cups, and utensils, lest the shared buffet consist of a dozen boxes of chocolate chip cookies and one veggie tray.

. . . .

Open circles offer an excellent opportunity to educate those who are new to the Craft while reminding the experienced of the special meaning of the ritual. Remember that these rituals may be the only Sabbats or Esbats some people ever attend, so strive to keep it enjoyable, educational, meaningful, succinct, and engaging.

Ann Moura *was raised in a family oral tradition of Green Witchcraft and has subsequently presented public rituals and taught about her Craft in workshops and seminars.*

Illustrator: Tim Foley

Necklace Numerology

Donald Tyson

Sometimes you may want a charm that does not look like a charm, so that you can wear it in plain sight all the time without having to sidestep questions about it. As you probably know, you cannot talk about the purpose for which a charm is made, or you will destroy the working of the charm. Hiding a charm in plain sight can be accomplished through something I call necklace numerology.

The charm, which is designed to achieve a specific purpose in life for the person who wears it, takes the form of a necklace of colored beads. This can be crafted as simply or as elaborately as desired, depending on the materials chosen. You will need a length of thread suitable for stringing the beads upon and a set of beads of the same size or similar sizes colored white, red, blue, green, and black.

Numerology involves the assigning of number values to letters of the alphabet. There are many ways of doing this, but the simplest assignment to the English alphabet is to write the letters in three rows, left to right, one row above the other, and associate a number from one to nine to each column in the rows. The result is that each number from 1 to 8 is linked with three letters, and the number 9 with two letters (there are 27 places in the three rows, but only 26 letters, so one of the places is left blank). This method is described in the 1912 numerological text *Numbers: Their Meaning and Magic* by Isidore Kozminsky, who describes it as a "new system of numeration."

The system divides the alphabet into three divisions or degrees. The first nine letters constitute the first degree, the next nine the second degree, and the last eight the third degree. Each letter is represented by a digit number, as follows:

Necklace Segment	1	2	3	4	5	6	7	8	9
Red, 1st degree	A	B	C	D	E	F	G	H	I
Blue, 2nd degree	J	K	L	M	N	O	P	Q	R
Green, 3rd degree	S	T	U	V	W	X	Y	Z	●

The nine numbers will correspond with the nine segments of the necklace, and the degree will correspond with the position within that segment. (Don't worry, this will make sense soon!)

For our purposes of charm making, each row of letters may be linked with one of three colors. A to I is assigned the color red, J to R the color blue, and S to Z the color green. The very last place, which has no letter, receives the color black, to signify the end. In this way the combination of a number and a color clearly indicate a letter of the alphabet. For example 5-red would be the letter E, and 7-green would be the letter Y.

The construction of our necklace charm is quite simple. Beads are arranged in nine sets of three from left to right. Each set of three beads is divided from the set next to it by a knot. Ten knots are enough to define and contain nine sets of three beads each. The white beads are merely placeholders, while colored beads indicate letters. A single black bead is placed at the end of the ninth segment on the far right to indicate the end of the necklace, so that it is not put on backwards by mistake.

Before we can make our necklace, we need to decide on our letters. To determine what letters are to be incorporated into our necklace charm, we must begin with our purpose. Each magic charm is made for one purpose, which may be specific or general, and may involve a single event in time or a continuing progression of events. Whatever the purpose, it must be clear enough in your mind to express in a single short sentence or phrase. Ideally the phrase should consist of from five to nine significant words—that is to say, meaningful words, not words such as *the* and *a* and *and*, which may be disregarded in making the charm.

The sentence or phrase must be expressed in the present tense, and must be positive. Avoid the use of negative words. Let us take as an example the purpose for the charm expressed by this sentence: "Love surrounds me and increases daily." This would be a charm to attract love of a general kind, not necessarily just romantic love. It would

result in a sustained loving environment. The key words of the sentence are five in number: *love, surrounds, me, increases, daily.* From these words, the first letters are selected: L, S, M, I, D.

The selection of the sentence or phrase is the most important part of the making of the charm. It is vital that you meditate on which words to choose and find the brief expression of meaning that most powerfully expresses your purpose for making the charm. If you have more than nine significant words, you must reduce the sentence until there are nine or fewer key words. It is best not to use less than five because otherwise the necklace will have a colorless appearance. If possible, avoid having the same key letter appear more than once. (If the same key letter does appear twice, both are represented by the same bead.)

The beads are knotted onto the necklace thread in order from left to right. In the above example, the letter S occupies the third place in the first segment. Tie a knot on the left side of the thread to act as a stop for the beads, and drop two white beads down on it as placeholders, then a single green bead to represent the S. It is green because the S is in third place in the segment. Tie a knot to end this first segment of the necklace. There are no letters in our charm from the second column, so drop three white beads down the thread to make the second segment, and tie a knot to end it. The letter L occupies the middle of the third segment so drop down a white bead, a blue bead, and a white bead. The key letter D is at the beginning and the key letter M is in the middle of the fourth segment, so the beads are red, blue, white. There are no key letters of the charm's purpose in the fifth segment, which receives three white beads. The six segment also gets three white beads, as does the seventh segment, and the eighth segment. The key letter I occurs in first place of the ninth segment, so the order of the beads is red, white, black (the final place of the ninth segment is always a black bead).

A J |S| B K |T| C L U|D| M V|E| N W|F| O X|G| P Y|H| Q Z|I| R ⊗

You may make this necklace charm as simply or as elaborately as you desire or as your craft skills permit. Instead of knots between the nine segments of the charm, you might prefer to use spacer beads or disks. This is fine, as long as the nine segments of three beads each are clearly distinguished. You may, if you wish, also add decorative beads on either side of the nine segments. Or you may string the beads on a fine chain of silver or gold rather than on a thread.

There is a redundancy in the construction of the necklace charm as described above. If twenty-seven beads are used in nine sets of three, it is possible to indicate each letter of the alphabet solely by position on the necklace—the colors red, blue, and green are not absolutely essential. Therefore, minimalists may prefer to construct the necklace charm using only white and black beads. A black bead is placed in each segment where a key letter of the phrase describing the purpose occurs. The final bead is always black and does not occupy the place of a letter, so no confusion arises from it. For example, the letter S in the first segment of the necklace could be indicated merely by a black bead in the third place in the segment—it is not really necessary to make this bead green, although using colored beads to indicate first, second, and third place in each segment livens up the appearance of the necklace, and makes its pattern a bit easier to distinguish.

It may be argued that the key letters of the sentence expressing the purpose of the charm are out of their proper order on the necklace. In the sentence they are ordered L, S, M, I, D; on the necklace they are ordered S, L, D, M, I. However, in making symbolic charms, it is not at all unusual for the key letters of a charm to be combined into a compound symbol composed of all the letters together that gives no indication of their correct order. The order of the letters is known to the person who has made the charm, and that is enough. No one else need know the order of the letters. This preserves the secrecy of the charm. Even if someone else understands the manner by which the necklace charm was constructed, and can identify the key letters of the purpose, it will be impossible for that person to determine the ordering of the key letters and/or the words that state the purpose of the charm.

To activate the charm, keep your purpose firmly in mind while making the necklace, and repeat to yourself the key phrase that expresses the purpose of the charm. After it has been completed, sit in a ritual circle and hold the necklace in your hands. Move your fingers over the beads from left to right, and identify in your mind the letters the colored beads stand for. Speak the letters aloud as you finger each colored bead in turn. Do not worry about the purpose at this point—it will already have been fixed into your subconscious mind during the making of the charm. Go over the beads on the necklace repeatedly from beginning to end, visualizing the letter each colored bead represents as you touch that bead with your fingers.

If the charm has been made for your own use, it is useful to repeat this telling of the beads on a regular basis. This will keep the charm charged and active. If it is made for someone else, you must infuse as much energy into the necklace as possible before giving it to the person for whom you have made it.

For more than three decades, **Donald Tyson** *has presented traditional systems of Western magic in ways that make sense to modern readers. It is his conviction that magic can be understood and used without the need to turn off the rational mind. His books span the full spectrum of the arcane arts, from scrying and Tarot reading, to astral projection and ritual spirit evocation. He lives in an old farm house in Nova Scotia, Canada, with his wife, Jenny, and his Siamese cat, Hermes.*

Illustrator: Rik Olson

Magical Transformations

Everything Old Is New Again

The Snow People

Linda Raedisch

The ancient Celts, we are told, divided the year into two halves: summer and winter. In Europe, the night of April 30 was both the last gasp of winter and the witches' last chance to party before the arrival of spring. And since witches were frightening to the medievals, I can't blame them for equating witches with winter. I'm not too fond of the season myself! It looks alright through the kitchen window, but who wants to go out in it? Even worse is the day after the storm when the glare of sunlight on hardened snow and the rasp of shovel on concrete announces that it's time to get up and out. It's business as usual in the ice-covered world. Our civilization makes few allowances for this most unforgiving of seasons.

If you don't love winter, it might give you courage to remember that modern humans were largely shaped by that most famous winter of all: the Ice Age. The Ice Age taught us to work together in quick-thinking groups to bring down woolly mammoths. And think of the organizational skills required to convert that mammoth into food, fuel, goods, and clothing.

The Ice Age must also have taught us some social skills that we have since lost. Imagine your entire extended family coming together for Thanksgiving. But instead of sharing a roof for a day or even a few days, you'll be enjoying one another's company for six months. It's too cold for the kids to play outside, and there's no cable. The only way, in my opinion, those families huddled together in their tricked-out rock shelters could have survived was by telling some really good stories. It may have been during those long Pleistocene winters that the kernels of our most powerful stories were born, if only because we needed their distraction so badly.

The only way, in my opinion, those families huddled together in their tricked-out rock shelters could have survived was by telling some really good stories.

For many of the Native Americans inhabiting the temperate zone, winter was the *only* time for telling stories. There were serious repercussions for breaking out the tales before the ground was frozen, not the least of which was the possibility that snakes and other creepy crawlies might sneak into bed with you. In Japan, on the other hand, the hot, humid summer is the time for telling snowy ghost stories. Why? To create shivers, of course! The Yuki Onna, or Snow Woman, is one such ghost. In some versions, she is a chaste young wife; in others, a supernaturally empowered harridan, but she is always terrifying enough to send a chill down the spine.

Let's take a tour around the world of snow creature tales of old…

The Snow Maiden (Russia)

Many readers will already be familiar with the tale of the Snow Maiden. It comes to us from Old Russia, a land of sparkling forests and frozen palaces. The tale begins, as do so many folktales the world over, with an old, childless couple. They are poor and devoutly religious (poverty and piety being *de riguer* for old childless couples in folktales). While cutting wood in the forest, they take a break to build a *snegourochka*, a little girl made of snowballs. Lo and behold, the snegourochka comes to life, and she is everything the old couple ever dreamed of in a daughter. She is pretty, respectful, and well dressed in fancy boots, cloak, and diamond tiara. She helps out around the house and, conveniently for her elderly parents, she's bypassed the diaper stage.

The storyteller would have us believe that this Snow Maiden is a

gift from God, a reward for the old couple's unwavering faith. Given the outcome of the story, however, the exercise seems cruel and pointless on God's part. For Snegourochka is not a child of flesh but of snow. In some versions of the story, she crumples at the first sign of spring. In others, she lasts until

Midsummer, only to be vaporized by the St. John's Day fires. A few writers hint at the possibility that, like Frosty, she'll be back again someday, but this is a modern gloss. When the girl is gone, she's gone, and the old couple is left with nothing but a soggy patch of forest floor.

No doubt it was a witch and not an angel hiding behind one of the snow-clad fir trees in the forest that day—perhaps Baba Yaga or one of those pesky German witches flown over from the west. "Be careful what you wish for," she might have cackled to herself as she worked her magic over the doomed little snegourochka.

Yuki Onna (Japan)

Another woodcutting foray brings us face to face with the Yuki Onna, the Japanese Woman of the Snows. No shrinking snowdrop here, the Yuki Onna is as ferocious as the Snow Maiden is sweet. In Lafcadio Hearn's retelling of the tale, it is man who invades the wild realm of the Yuki Onna and suffers the consequences.

On their way home with their loads of wood, teenage Minokichi and the elderly Mosaku are stranded on the wrong side of the river by a snow storm. They find shelter in a tiny boathouse but have no means of lighting a fire. Old Mosaku soon falls asleep. Losing his battle against the cold, Minikichi also sleeps, but only for an instant. He wakes to see a white-clad woman breathing cold white smoke over the sleeping Mosaku. To the younger man's horror, the spirit is about to do the same to Minokichi, but she pauses and he is able to look up into her starkly beautiful face. The Yuki Onna spares him on account of his youth and because she has taken a shine to him. But she warns him to tell no one what he has seen; if he does, she will kill him.

Minokichi survives the night, just barely, while Mosaku is frozen to death. Minokichi tells himself this Woman of the Snows was

probably just a hallucination. He goes on with his life as a woodcutter and thinks no more of the strange apparition.

The next winter, he meets a pretty girl on the forest path. Her name is O-Yuki. Long story short, they become husband and wife. O-Yuki bears her woodcutter ten children, but mysteriously does not age a day.

At last, in the candlelight one evening, thick-as-a-brick Minokichi notices a resemblance between the ageless O-Yuki and the spirit he thought he saw all those years ago. He tells O-Yuki everything, thus breaking his promise to the Yuki Onna. Never mind that they're one and the same—O-Yuki/Yuki Onna is livid. This time, it is for the sake of the children that she spares Minokichi's life. She threatens the bewildered woodcutter once more with death if he does not take proper care of the little ones, then she disappears.

This is, thanks to Hearn, the most famous version of the Yuki Onna story, but it is not the only one. In another variation set down by Victorian world-traveler and collector of tales, Richard Gordon Smith, the Yuki Onna is a ghost in the more usual sense: she is the spirit of a young woman named Oyasu who died in a snowstorm. On the eve of the anniversary of her death, Oyasu presents herself not to her own family but to an old widower named Kyuzaemon.

Poor Kyuzaemon bars the door against the unearthly stranger only to turn around and see her standing next to his bed. She has long hair, a pretty face, and the signature white kimono. She explains to Kyuzaemon that she wishes to stay only until the wind dies down. As a spirit, she's able to fly, so presumably the storm has only blown her off course. She was, in fact, on her way to visit her husband-in-life, Isaburo, who was also her father's adopted son. She is going to persuade him to return to her father's house to care for the old man in his dotage.

Oyasu is a polite house guest, as far as ghosts go. She pays her respects at Kyuzaemon's ancestral altar. Then, as soon as the storm abates, she goes on her way. The next morning, Kyuzaemon heads to the neighboring village to confirm her story. Yes, Oyasu did indeed appear to Isaburo in the night and convince him to return to his adoptive father's house. To lend an air of truth to the event, Smith informs us that it took place on January 19, 1833.

In the northwest of Japan, where this story was collected, those who met their deaths in

In the northwest of Japan ... those who met their deaths in snow were believed to persist as snow ghosts, flying silently over the frozen landscape, haunting those left behind.

snow were believed to persist as snow ghosts, flying silently over the frozen landscape, haunting those left behind. For some reason, it is only women, like Oyasu, who live on in legend.

Snow Boy (Lenape)

To meet a male snow spirit, we travel to the mid-Atlantic. New Jersey (along with parts of Delaware, Pennsylvania, and New York) is Snow Boy territory, for this is the ancestral home of the peoples now known as the Lenape or Delaware. The tale of Snow Boy is unique to them.

According to the story, Snow Boy's mother was very young when he was born, and her child's paternity was a mystery. When other children upset him, the little boy had the habit of putting their fingers in his mouth and sucking them until they turned black from frostbite. By his own account, his name was "Snow and Ice."

Then, one day in early spring, Snow Boy announced to his fellow villagers that he had to be moving on. Though he never named his father, he said he had been sent from the sky in order to show his mother's people how to track both game and enemies. When the winter came, he told them, he would return in the form of the falling snowflakes.

Down by the river, he asked to be placed on an ice floe. The people obliged him, placing beside him a birch bark container full of *kahamakun* (see below) and off he went. He returns every year, just as promised. Lenape Indians living in Oklahoma re-enacted this ritual into the twentieth century, though presumably with smaller chunks of ice. Snow Boy never again appeared to his people as a human child, but he was still given his portion of kahamakun and bid a fond farewell.

Kahamakun is parched, or dried, white corn that has been toasted over the embers of a fire or in a cast iron skillet. The corn

is then pounded, sifted and mixed with maple sugar. This was the favorite snack of hunters on the go because it was easy to carry and packed with carbohydrates. Because the corn had already been toasted, it could be prepared with either hot or cold water. That way, the hunters could eat quickly, devoting all their energy and attention to tracking the deer over the white blanket Snow Boy had laid upon the ground.

Resources

Bierhorst, John, ed. *The White Deer and Other Stories Told by the Lenape*. New York: William Morrow, 1995.

Harrington, M. R. *The Indians of New Jersey: Dickon among the Lenapes*. New Brunswick, NJ: Rutgers University Press, 1966.

Haviland, Virginia. *Favorite Fairy Tales Told in Russia*. Boston: Little, Brown and Company, 1961.

Hearn, Lafcadio. *Kwaidan: Stories and Studies of Strange Things*. New York: Dover, 1968.

Seiki, Keigo, ed., translated by Richard J. Adams. *Folktales of Japan*. Chicago: The University of Chicago Press, 1963.

Smith, Richard Gordon. *Ancient Tales and Folklore of Japan*. London: A & C Black, 1908.

Zvorykin, Boris. *The Firebird and Other Russian Fairy Tales*. New York: The Viking Press, 1978.

When not concocting recipes, **Linda Raedisch** *writes about holidays, obscure traditions, and witches of all sorts. She continues to live in northern New Jersey, despite the long winters.*

Illustrator: Bri Hermanson

Being the Change

Tess Whitehurst

The year 2012 is finally here, and it's lived up to its promise of marking an uncommonly interesting moment in the history of our species. To many of us, it appears that we're at a critical juncture, which may very soon culminate in one of two main outcomes: we humans might destroy or decimate ourselves by blowing ourselves up or making our environment unlivable, or we might find a way to harmoniously evolve into a peaceful and mutually beneficial relationship with our planet and each other.

You must be the change you want to see in the world.
—MAHATMA GANDHI

While it remains to be seen whether or not this big change is true, it is nonetheless significant that so many people, regardless of their spiritual and/or scientific persuasion, have a strong feeling that it is. Furthermore, no matter what the future may or may not hold, moving toward greater harmony is never a bad thing, and there has never been a better time for it than now.

As shapers of reality, our role during this time is extremely vital: our thoughts, words, rituals, and visualizations, when directed toward universal healing and harmonization, have the potential to be a precious contribution to the future of the human race, wildlife, and the environment as we know it. In addition to our work in the ethereal or spiritual realm, working in the physical realm—as activists, disseminators of information, artists, healers, teachers, volunteers, etc.—can fortify our efforts, empower our intentions, and generally help heal the world in a concrete, tangible way. And, as we know from the Law of Returns, each of our positive intentions and generous actions will return to us multiplied, so our global healing efforts will also allow us to steep ourselves in positivity, harmony, and good fortune.

All You Need Is Love

In 1967, the BBC asked the Beatles to perform for the first live, *global* television broadcast ever. In response, John Lennon wrote and the Beatles performed "All You Need is Love." It's said that it was watched in thirty-one countries simultaneously, by 400 million people. Needless to say, this was an unfathomably powerful act of magic. Even now, more than forty years later, not a day goes by without this song playing on radio stations all over the world.

While few of us will appear on national television in our lifetime (let alone an international broadcast), like pebbles creating concentric ripples across a lake, we all have the capacity to project

positive energy and etheric broadcasts on a similar scale. To do so, we must begin with ourselves. We must love ourselves dearly and forgive ourselves for our faults. Then, we must love and forgive those around us. Finally, we must do our best to love and forgive the entire world. Once we allow ourselves to do this, we create exponential positive change in the present and for the future, simply by dwelling in the world. Not only that, but we naturally want to engage in activities that help and heal, not out of a sense of obligation or martyrdom, but as a natural expression of our innermost essence.

I know I just made it all sound terribly simple and easy, and that's because in truth it is. But of course, we all know it doesn't always start out that way, and it definitely doesn't always feel that way. Before we even begin, we've got to rise above our cultural training to loathe ourselves, to feel bitter toward or slighted by the world, and to complain about how unfair everything seems to be. Then, we've got to make an effort to maintain a positive outlook despite any seemingly horrific or generally undesirable conditions we may observe in our present lives and in the world around. Only by doing so can we help to manifest conditions that are more in alignment with love and less in alignment with fear. To do this, it's imperative that we do our very best to keep our vibrations clean, clear, and protected through meditation, prayer, visualization, and energetic cleansing and protection.

We must establish new inner programming by reminding ourselves of the truth again and again: love is all, all is love, and love is all we need.

Additionally and simultaneously, we must establish new inner programming by reminding ourselves of the truth again and again: that love is all, all is love, and love is all we need. You might even post the profound words of Lennon's "All You Need Is Love" near your workspace or altar and inwardly repeat them in the morning, before bed, and whenever else you feel it necessary.

Watering the Seeds of Genius

There is a seed of genius in your heart. It is a seed with the potential for bringing about more healing and creating more positive change than you can possibly imagine, and it is unlike any other seed in any other heart. In order to allow this seed to begin to sprout, you must quiet your mind, shut out the noise and illusions of the world, let your heart open, and listen to the wisdom deep within. Then, you must water the seed and seedling with patience, open-mindedness, and a commitment to following your inner nudges.

If the Beatles had devoted their lives to helping people with leprosy in Calcutta, "All You Need is Love" would never have worked its magic on the world. Similarly, if Mother Teresa had pursued a music career, countless lives would have suffered from her absence. While these are exceptionally famous examples, one need not be even the tiniest bit famous to set in motion potent waves of positivity and healing. All one needs is to be true to her heart and follow the path of her joy.

Whether we're called to volunteer, to contribute, to engage in a traditional service-based career, or to engage in any other action that allows us to be of service to the world, being the change we wish to see is a necessary ingredient to living passionately, purposefully, and with deep and abiding joy.

Tapping Into the Divine

When it comes to "being the change," what better way to start than by tapping into our divine guidance? As Pagans, our spirituality is by definition kaleidoscopic and inclusive, so we have a lot of potential inspiration to draw on. Connecting with one or more of the following deities might be an excellent jumping off point. When reading the descriptions below, if you feel an energetic boost, emotional charge, or immediate sense of excitement or joy, you've found the trailhead to your path! Spend some quality time with that divinity in meditation, ritual, and dreamtime, and then follow your intuition about how to "be the change" by staying positive, radiating acceptance and love, and/or taking action in the physical world. You might also place an image of your chosen deity or deities on your altar, or assemble an altar with the specific intention to align with your most ideal path of joyful service.

Archangel Michael

Michael is a powerful protector who removes negativity and negative influences while providing a swift energetic infusion of confidence and courage. He's not only known for assisting those who put themselves in physical harm's way for the sake of others, such as police officers and military personnel, but he also helps those of us who do healing and protection work in the subtle realms, such as energy workers, intuitive counselors, and therapists. His energy is blindingly bright and glowing, and he carries a sword of light that cuts through, purifies, and removes cords of ignorance, attachment, fear, and negativity in all forms. You can also ask him to protect you or others with an encompassing sphere of very bright white or indigo light.

Artemis

If you feel drawn to help adolescent girls embrace their maidenness and womanhood, to empower women, to protect animals and/or the environment, or to engage in midwifery, prenatal yoga, or any other practice that is concerned with birthing or the female reproductive system, Artemis just might be your girl. She challenges the meaning of the word *feminine* by embodying its fiercest aspects: protectiveness, independence, and strength.

The Faerie Realm

The realm of Faerie is a vast and multi-faceted place, and one can spend a lifetime exploring it. Tapping into its energy and getting to know the landscape and the beings who populate it can be very helpful, especially to those of us who are artists of any kind, work with and feel a connection to children, feel motivated to fight

for human rights and sexual freedom, or are passionate about the welfare of animals and the environment.

How can I best serve the world? How can I turn the tide of my consciousness from despair to hope and from fear to love?

We can visit the Faerie Realm in meditation and in the dream state, and because it's parallel to our realm, we can learn to perceive it at certain times when we are outdoors—especially in (pesticide-free) gardens and natural settings. One way to begin to do this is by relaxing and tuning into a blossoming plant or a tree. Mentally ask questions of the plant spirit, such as "How can I best serve the world?" or "How can I turn the tide of my consciousness from despair to hope, and from fear to love?" Then, simply allow yourself to receive the answers as a feeling or deep inner knowing.

FORSETI

Forseti, the Norse god of justice, is an excellent helper to those of us concerned with fairness, such as lawyers, judges, lobbyists, lawmakers, and activists. When you call on him, he can speedily infuse your cause with positive energy and (provided you are in the right) help tip the scales in your favor.

HECATE

Some people—such as doctors, nurses, funeral directors, grief counselors, mediums, spirit clearers, and clergy—are called to help ease and foster the transition between this realm and the next. The goddess Hecate can help support us in these efforts, as she rules the threshold and crossroads between life and the afterlife. She helps us to meet and greet our fears surrounding death so that we can approach it, and help others approach it, with grace and courage. So many people are crippled by a fear of death, and so much of the world's violence and confusion is based upon this fear. With Hecate's assistance, we can begin to alleviate this fear and help to bring about a deeper level of universal peace and harmony.

LAKSHMI

Lakshmi, the beautiful Hindu goddess of wealth, reminds us that in truth, this is an abundant universe with plenty for everyone. She can be a wonderful helper for people who want to bring greater wealth, affluence, and prosperity consciousness to those most in need of it. When tuning into Lakshmi's energy, you might listen with your intuitive ear to the jingling coins that surround her and look with your intuitive sight at the flowing river of abundance at her feet.

ST. FRANCIS

Perhaps you are drawn to help protect the animals and to raise the awareness of humans to help change the way animals are treated on this planet. If so, St. Francis wants to assist you. Although St. Francis is a famous Catholic saint, if you spend any time with him, you'll find that he's actually a Pagan at heart. One of the amazing ways that St. Francis channeled divine wisdom during his lifetime was through his writings, which include the following proverb about animals:

Not to hurt our humble brethren
is our first duty to them, but to stop there is not enough.
We have a higher mission:
to be of service to them whenever they require it.

When all humans can consciously align themselves with divine wisdom, we will be blessed with an unprecedented level of peace. White Buffalo Calf Woman is a beautiful Lakota deity with the mission of connecting our human consciousness with the infinite consciousness of the Great Spirit for the purpose of establishing true and lasting peace. We all want peace on Earth, but if you are strongly drawn to help establish it, especially through spiritual means, you might try calling on White Buffalo Calf Woman for help.

RESOURCES:

St. Francis of Assisi. "Not to Hurt." *Environmental Ethics: An Anthology.* Ed. Andrew Light and Holmes Rolston III. Oxford: Blackwell Publishers, Ltd, 2003. 66.

Kaltreider, Kurt. *American Indian Prophecies.* Carlsbad, CO: Hay House, 1998.

Virtue, Doreen. *Archangels and Ascended.* Carlsbad, CO: Hay House, 2004.

Tess Whitehurst *is the author of* Magical Housekeeping: Simple Charms and Practical Tips for Creating a Harmonious Home *and* The Good Energy Book: Creating Harmony & Balance for Yourself & Your Home. *She's also an intuitive counselor, feng shui consultant, and columnist for* Witches and Pagans *magazine. Her website (www .tesswhitehurst.com) and e-newsletter (Good Energy) feature simple rituals, meditations, and musings for everyday magical living. Tess lives in Venice Beach, CA, with two magical cats, one musical boyfriend, and a constant stream of visiting hummingbirds.*

Illustrator: Kathleen Edwards

Reclaiming the Wise Woman and Cunning Man

Paniteowl

The Craft is currently experiencing a rebirth, and the growing pains this entails can truly be uncomfortable. Trying to reconnect with the ways of our ancestors can be difficult given the scarcity of information in many cultures. It's hard enough to remember things we observed in childhood, and then taking another look, try to put situations into context from our adult perspective. Sometimes, we lose things in the translation. Now extrapolate those difficulties remembering your own past to try to recall our cultural past from centuries ago. Reclaiming the nature of the Wise Woman and the Cunning Man of old takes a lot of research and development!

Anthropologists, archeologists, and geologists can all help re-create a situation in a specific locality. They can carbon date fossils, explain the layers of dirt and stone, and even tell us what kinds of tools were used by indigenous people. But they can't tell us how those people lived, laughed, loved, worked, and survived without using imagination and the personal experiences of today's world. Our own egos will overlay all of the opinions, no matter what the physical evidence indicates.

Recent history is very dependent upon written articles that give us glimpses into the thoughts, hopes, and fears of those who have gone before us. Whether it is an old newspaper or a letter found wrapped in ribbons in an old abandoned attic, our interest is piqued by the insights we get about a real person. Historical facts are necessary to write our history as a people, but personal knowledge of someone who lived long before will always grab our interest and make the dry facts of history much more appealing.

When attempting to reclaim our history of the Craft, we should be looking at the biographies of our predecessors. However, once we go beyond the last few hundred years, we run into a blank wall of propaganda and fear mongering. We are left with a hunger for the true knowledge of the Old Ways, with no real assurance that our impressions and suppositions are valid.

What we can surmise from our own experience is simply that real people, living real lives, survived and accomplished many wonders that seem beyond natural human capabilities. I would love to reclaim their strength and perseverance in what must have been an environment of great adversity, but, to be truthful, I don't want to return to the "Olde Days." I don't want to go back to a time of hardship. I'm a modern witch—I like indoor plumbing, central heat,

public transportation, and grocery stores stocked with food. I like cell phones, computers, digital music, and public libraries. So why am I fascinated with the ways of the Wise Women and Cunning Men? Because they were the "experts" of their day in knowing how to live well within their environments. We are the ones who need to understand the whys and hows of their Craft so we can emulate their example by living within our own experiences. We can become the Wise Woman or the Cunning Man by being knowledgeable and aware of our environment and being willing to become a mentor in our community.

A Cunning Man would have been consulted as to where the herds may be before going on a hunt to provide food. He'd also be an authority on weaponry and supplies needed to make the journey.

He would encourage people to practice their skills before setting off on the hunt and would help to train the young by example and through the telling of stories of previous hunts. He would encourage the concepts of achievement and self-awareness. He would be the coach, the trainer, and the father figure to those who would someday lead the tribe or clan. He would give his knowledge and experience to those who would take his place as the Elder, or Cunning Man. He would ensure the survival of his species. In today's world, the Cunning Man would be a mentor, helping the young find jobs, get an education, and look forward to raising a family with pride and self-assurance.

The Wise Woman would be consulted on almost every level of everyday life. From healing herbs to preparing skins for clothing, all tribe members would seek her advice. Her skills were necessary for the health and welfare of her people. Could she also offer sympathetic magic spells to aid people? Of course, just as the Cunning Man would use symbols of the animals they needed to hunt for survival.

The Wise Woman may have been someone who knew how to prepare the foods taken on the hunt. She may have been the one who taught the children to chew the skins in order to make them pliable so that they could be made into clothing. She may have been the one who healed the sick with her recipes and potions. She may have been the one to give advice to the lovelorn. Today you would find her among the caregivers, the teachers, and the mentors. The

Wise Woman most definitely would be the mid-wife who was consulted on all aspects of pregnancy. A woman who needed help because she was unable to get pregnant or had many miscarriages would have sought her advice as to what to eat, how to act, and what not to do. The woman with too many children or the girl who was too young to carry a child would consult with her on ways to prevent a pregnancy.

The Cunning Man and the Wise Woman positions in the tribes were absolutely necessary for survival. Those who could read the signs and work with Earth were respected guides within the framework of the Clan or Tribe. From their input and their ability to give good advice came the modern world we now inhabit. We are the descendants of survivors.

However, we still need those mentors and advisors. Today we have many more opportunities to seek out and receive advice about the vast complexities of our world. Today it is even more important that we emulate the Wise Women and Cunning Men of the past, who used their knowledge of their own environment to enhance life and support their community.

Do we need a Wise Woman to find out when the buses run? Nope, we simply need to pick up a schedule. Do we need a Cunning Man to tell us where to go for sushi? Nah, we simply check the phone book or use an Internet search engine. However, given human nature, we often ask a friend rather than doing our own research. The age-old habit of asking for advice from people we know and trust will always be part of how we "survive" in the world today. We need mentoring more than ever before. We need the "expert" to give advice in any number of situations.

If we are ill, we do need to see a medical practitioner. We may go to our family doctor or walk into a clinic. We allow them to examine us, and then we decide whether to take their advice or not. We may decide to get another opinion or seek an alternative method of healing. Healthy people have access to a great deal of knowledge as to what we should eat, how we should exercise, and how we should take care of ourselves. Do we always heed this advice? No, but we do have *access* to it. It is our responsibility to get smart about our own bodies.

In the past, it was the responsibility of the individual to contribute to the tribe. Planting a field, tending a herd, tanning a skin, and blacksmithing were all sought-after skills. Today we depend on the grocery store, the clothing store, or the local hardware store. But we have to use our skills to make the money in order to get the things we need. So we need education to get a job! Our public education system offers a wide variety of disciplines where we can find our niche and build a life's work that fulfills us. Teachers are the mentors who give us the opportunities for learning. We can see that these professions have taken over much of the teaching duties of the Wise Woman/Cunning Man, just as the modern medical profession has taken on the tasks of healing. The skills of the Wise Woman and Cunning Man are still being practiced today as a necessity in the larger societies of the modern world.

We can all recognize the advantage of having this type of knowledge available to us, but we also know, through experience, that even the most learned professional may lack common sense or "street smarts." These skills are just as valid for survival today as they were in ancient times. The professionals who are out of touch with their clients or co-workers may be technically proficient yet dismally inept at recognizing the human nature of those around them. They may forget, or never been made aware of, the fact that human nature is definitely part of the environment.

A witch may be a doctor, a lawyer, or an educator. We use our skills within our profession, but we also carry with us the added awareness of our environment to enhance these skills. We must carry on the tradition of the Wise Woman and Cunning Man by using the knowledge necessary and available to us and incorporating the ancient ways by weaving the Craft of the Wise into our everyday lives.

A witch may be a cashier at the market, a volunteer fire person, a police officer, or a dog walker—it doesn't matter how one makes a living. What does matter is how we reclaim the sense of the Wise Woman or Cunning Man by being aware of our environment. Developing our "street smarts" is an age-old way of surviving well.

Seeking, giving, and heeding advice is a personal choice. It includes being responsible for your own thoughts, words, and deeds. Reclaiming the responsibility of the Wise Woman and Cunning

Man is something many people overlook in their search for the magic that comes with the position. Reclaiming the Craft of the Wise also means being trustworthy and able to trust those from whom you seek advice. The best teachers are those we can look up to. Our role models today are those who live by example and show us the ways of survival regardless of current difficulties.

We don't have to reach back in history trying to re-create an environment that is no longer valid in today's society. We don't need a man to tell us where to hunt or a woman to show us how to fashion clothes from skins. What we need to do is reclaim the essence of the Wise Woman and the Cunning Man. We need to emulate their nature as they struggled, experimented, and found ways to help their tribe survive. We need to recognize that the Wise Woman and Cunning Man are alive and well in today's society. They are still our best role models as the survivors of whatever environmental conflicts are tossed in our path. What they know is simply that our environment includes human nature with all its foibles. We can reclaim that knowledge and act accordingly. We are not separate from our environment, but vital participants in its development.

Paniteowl, *simply known as Owl to many in the Pagan Community, has been a familiar face at festivals and gatherings. Over the past two decades she has been a popular presenter, giving workshops and organizing events throughout the East Coast and Canada. Her articles and poetry have been featured in many periodicals and on Internet sites. She and her husband have a 56-acre woodlot in the mountains of northeast Pennsylvania, where they have hosted annual gatherings for Pagans twice a year for the past 15 years. Owl also moderates a number of Internet groups, focusing on the Solitary practitioners, as well as Wicca Covened, and Non-Wicca practitioners who want to keep in touch with the wider Pagan community.*

Illustrator: Tim Foley

Hibernation:
Embracing Winter

Susan Pesznecker

What does winter make you think of? Playing in the snow? Fires in the fireplace? Pots of tea and cozy afternoons spent reading? Working on magickal projects? For some, the winter months are filled with homey, comforting images, and we look forward to pulling on wool sweaters and making up the beds in flannel sheets. But others regard winter with deep foreboding. For victims of Seasonal Affective Disorder (SAD), the dark days of winter may trigger depression, sleeplessness, and a loss of energy. The incidence of SAD is on the rise.

Although the disorder is typically thought to be related to a reduction in sunlight during the winter months, many now believe that it could also be deeply connected to a human failure to "hibernate."

In millennia past, humans lived from day to day, surviving through subsistence. As hunter-gatherers, their lives depended on their ability to find and store the food and materials they needed to survive. Forced to travel from place to place to follow natural cycles and animal migrations, their lives were tenuous. A particularly severe winter, a slight climactic change, a missing accustomed food source, or the chance death of a critical adult could wipe out an entire tribe. These Stone Age people constantly flirted with bad weather, hypothermia, and starvation as well as trying not to be eaten by a tertiary carnivore—humans were decidedly not high on the food chain back then.

As time went on, humans learned to use tools, make fire, and communicate with more ease. With these new skills, life became less tenuous. Instead of seasonal wildcrafting, Neolithic humans learned to grow the plants they needed. In addition to place-specific hunting, they learned to raise and use animals. Fire was started with flint and steel instead of laborious friction. Illnesses were treated with medicinal herbs. Warm clothing from animal skins offered realistic protection from the elements, and stone tools made every task easier. With these modern improvements came increased life expectancy and perhaps a bit of time to kick back and enjoy life a little.

Stone Age living revolved around the seasons, and early religions honored Earth's bounty and gave thanks for the gifts of weather, food, and life itself. Foods were tightly connected to the season: greens were enjoyed in the spring, berries in the summer, root vegetables in the fall, and dried stores  in the winter. Daily life was governed by tasks and activities that tied in to the current season. Planting and new births happened in the spring. Summer featured long hot days in which to accomplish many tasks, such as drying food, killing and skinning animals, weaving cloth, and gathering berries. Autumn meant time to hunt, harvest, and store food.

And then came winter.

In winter, the ancients retreated to their caves and hunkered down. Wrapped in their warmest skins, they built fires against the cold, baked breads, and ate from pots of stews and soups that simmered over the fire. It was too cold to go outside, so they remained indoors and passed the time, perhaps weaving baskets, working leather, or forming tools from flint and obsidian. The people probably told stories, recounting hunts or other important events. Perhaps the clan's knowledge keeper would recount history in traditional oral fashion. They may have sung songs, enjoyed games, or even enacted mock hunts around the fire. And they would pray, in their fashion, for the return of warmth and the return of the light, which was believed to happen at the whim of the gods.

Winter was a dangerous time for the people. Enough food had to be put away to get them through the winter, and even with food stores, starvation was a constant threat. The weather was a hazard, too. Fuel had to be gathered in milder months to furnish warmth throughout the long, cold months. Enough animals must be hunted to provide warm skins and furs. Dried plants and raw materials created a store for medicines, storage containers, tools, weapons, clothes, and housing.

The tribe survived through cooperation. They dressed warmly, ate high-fat foods, and passed the days communally. Light was limited, so when light was sufficient they worked at their tasks, and when it was too dark to work, they slept. The reduced activity and extra sleep conserved energy, reduced caloric expenditure, and protected such valuable resources as food and fuel. Their lives during those cold, dark months mimicked a state of voluntary hibernation. They respected the winter, understood what it meant to their lives, and adapted accordingly, and they did this even though they feared that the dark cold nights might never end. When spring came, they emerged from their winter cocoons to greet the softly greening Earth, the first buds of plants emerging from the still-cold ground. They gave thanks for the return of light, the return of warmth, the return of the world's fertility for yet another cycle in the Wheel of Life.

That was then. This is now.

Let's look at our lives today. In many locations, there is little or no seasonal variation—and as our planet gradually warms, even those variations may be diminishing. For some, spring brings the urge to garden. Summer may mean vacation, sunscreen, and the kids being home from school. Autumn is time to put away the lawn chairs, carve a pumpkin, and exchange shorts for jeans. But many have

lost touch with the simple rhythms of Earth and the turning of the seasonal wheel.

We "modern humans" do things when we want and how we want. Technology has allowed us to manipulate the environment so we can continue working, playing, or doing whatever we feel like doing in any month and at any time of the day or night. If we want to work when it's dark, we turn on lights. We've even invented daylight saving time to provide brighter mornings and longer days. If we're hot in August, we flip on the air conditioning. If we're cold in January, we crank up the heat. If we're hungry for raspberries in November, we can buy fresh ones, probably imported from Chile. We indulge in spray-on tans, mimicking summer even when it's not. Some people are so anxious to avoid winter they bisect their lives, spending the cold half of the year in Florida or taking beach vacations in February. In short, many live their lives based on what they want at the moment and what technology has provided to them, but they seem to have lost awareness of or respect for Earth's normal cycles. It's no wonder our internal date books are confused!

Seasonal Affective Disorder occurs when people with normal energy and mood experience low energy, fatigue, and depressive symptoms during the winter months. The long-accepted theory is that SAD is primarily a light-dependent disorder. It's often treated with light therapy, melatonin, and other therapies that more or less simulate the sleep-wake-activity cycles associated with the summer months.

As a Pagan and someone whose daily life is Earth-centered, I've always believed—and science is beginning to support me—that SAD may result at least in part from the failure to observe the annual cycles and the season of winter. It may result from denying what we're really "supposed" to be doing during the dark months: yielding to a deep, instinctive awareness of winter and its special rhythms. Simply said, I think that much of SAD results from a failure to hibernate.

To hibernate means to spend the winter in a dormant state. When animals hibernate, their metabolism is depressed: their vital signs slow, temperature drops, kidney function diminishes, and they appear to sleep deeply, rousing now and then for a bite of food. The word *hibernation* is also used figuratively to describe a person who remains inactive or indoors for an extended period for an extended period of time. Humans are not known to hibernate in the literal sense—with actual changes in metabolism and level of consciousness—although recent studies have identified hibernation triggers that appear to send humans into a hibernation-like condition, which scientists believe may be useful in treating serious injuries or in long-duration space travel (Harlow). In their book, *Why We Get Sick*, evolutionary biologists Randolph Nesse and George Williams talk about the remnant of hibernative response in humans and suggest that SAD may indeed be a mal-adaptive response to seasonal change.

Connections between human energy, behavior, and seasonal changes are well-established. We have no problems ramping up our activity level and spending more time outdoors when summer arrives. But at the time of year when darkness is upon us and when our instincts (and the available light) tell us to conserve energy by staying indoors and cutting back our daily routine, we continue to maintain our usual schedules almost as if ignoring winter's arrival. The vast majority of American adults work eight hours a day, five days a week for fifty or fifty-one weeks out of the year. The schedule doesn't change from season to season. One day is pretty much like another. Thus, at a time of year when the psyche aches to sit around the fire, engage in small but important tasks, and slow down, we're pressured to keep up the established routine. In a season traditionally set aside for rest and hibernation, we might do everything *but* rest. This, in itself, can create a depressed mood if one interprets the normal winter slow-down as something unpleasant or unhealthy. Instead of accepting winter as a normal, seasonal part in their lives, many people lament against the short days and dark nights, rebel against the ebbing of energy, and regard these normal feelings as symptoms of ill health. This type of emotional stress is not only self-perpetuating but can easily lead to actual physical or emotional illness.

Our diet is always an important aspect of supporting health and vitality, and this may be especially important during winter. At a time of year when people normally gain a few pounds (an ancient throw-back to the necessity of adding body fat to guard against starvation), and when we would normally subsist on baked root

vegetables, homemade breads, soups, stews, preserved foods, etc., winter finds many people continuing to eat as if it was summertime. We can go to the local market and find imported fresh fruit, seasonal farmed fish, and hothoused baby greens twelve months out of the year. We don't have to worry about gathering or preserving food because we can buy whatever we want whenever we want it. Now, let's be clear: I love the taste of a good strawberry as much as the next person, but in most parts of the world, we aren't meant to be eating fresh, ripe strawberries in January! This modern, uberaccess to seasonally inappropriate foods may be helping us ignore the reality of winter.

The research I've done suggests that SAD may be related to or influenced by the failure to show an instinctual awareness of Earth's cyclic year: specifically, by the failure to hibernate properly. Ignoring winter's routines in one's daily life sets up a tremendous internal conflict. While our genes and centuries of tradition scream at us to slow down and hunker around the fire, the modern world and its expectations scream even louder at us to keep going!

I've served as my own guinea pig in investigating these ideas. Several years back, I began making a conscious effort to "observe winter" as fully as I could. I'm someone who has always loved winter, but even I noticed the ebb of energy and sometimes a slight displeasure at not being able to do everything I wanted to be doing. Once I had formulated my theories on the problems of failed hibernation, I dug into winter in earnest. Retreating to my own house (cave) with my loved ones during the dark months, I cut back on my social schedule and on externally imposed routines. I began going to bed earlier and found that it felt good. I used fewer lights in the house, leaving lights on only in the rooms I was in and dimming those when I could. I lit more hearth fires and worked by candle and lamplight when I could, and I soon found that the soft lights created a wondrously comforting mood that traditional lighting missed altogether. In the evenings, I invited friends and family to join me in quiet pastimes: cross-stitch, reading, and so on. (And yes—some television too. No one's perfect!) We visited and played games and shared stories. I tackled a couple of big magickal projects: a deep study of runes and the staged crafting of a hiking staff. One of the most concrete changes I made was absolute adherence to a winter diet, which meant emphasizing foods that were naturally available (either fresh in my area or stocked in my own pantry) during the winter months. On weekends, I simmered a kettle of soup and baked a loaf or two of bread. Meals were supplemented with dried grains and legumes and with pies and cobblers of preserved or dried fruits. Sometimes we'd actually cook in the fireplace, which was lots of fun. On less frigid days, I'd take long walks, observing the winter around me and rejoicing in snow days.

I noticed an astounding change in my overall mood and energy level after making these simple changes. The feeling of continually fighting off "winter doldrums" vanished.

The results? As someone who already enjoyed winter, I noticed an astounding change in my overall mood and energy level after making these simple changes. The feeling of continually fighting off "winter doldrums" vanished, and I felt myself embracing the rhythms of the cooking fire, darkness, dense foods, and low light. When I did my best to actively observe winter, I was filled with a quiet sense of rightness and of being in tune with Earth. I felt happier, more relaxed, and much more effective with my magickal practices.

I'd like to share some specific guidelines for following the seasonal wheel and doing a proper job of winter hibernation. <u>Note</u>: *For anyone who has been diagnosed with clinical depression or SAD, my suggestions do not constitute medical recommendations, and I would encourage you to discuss these ideas with your physician before trying them. Likewise, if you're taking medication for SAD, please do not stop the medication without advice from your health care provider.*

Prepare yourself magickally. The month of January is ruled by Janus, Roman guardian of doorways, gates, and thresholds. Often pictured with two or three faces, Janus can see into the past and future simultaneously. Consider winter as a threshold or gate to the coming year. Carry out a ritual that welcomes winter and proclaims your personal and magickal plans and intentions. In most traditions, winter is associated with the north and the earth element, making it an excellent time for grounding, centering, and energy work. A pine, cedar, or sage smudge is a powerful way to cleanse or purify as often as needed.

Adjust your schedule. Simply said, do less. Don't overcommit, and respect the season's slower pace. Focus activities on the home front. Now is the time to settle into books, projects, and other activities that require a long span of time. Have family game nights or invite friends over to share the fun.

Adjust your environment. Invest in good lead-free candles for atmosphere, and if you have a fireplace, stock up on dry, seasoned wood. Light the area you're living or working in, but leave lights off through the rest of the house. Turn the thermostat down to 65 degrees—leave blanket throws on chairs and couches, and wear slippers to keep your feet warm and layers of fleece or wool sweaters for toastiness. Make your bed with flannel sheets and thick blankets and spreads.

Purify your surroundings. Many houseplants are valuable for purifying the air, particularly peace lilies, rubber plants, and spider plants. You might also invest in an air purifier for the bedroom and main living spaces. On warmer days, open the doors and windows to let fresh air in.

Embrace winter herbs and spices. Burn incense or diffuse oils in scents of cinnamon, clove, cardamom, pine, or cedar. Sip herbal teas or fresh-made Chai. Simmer a kettle of hot cider or mulled wine with fresh ginger, cinnamon sticks, star anise, whole cloves, cardamom pods, and thin slices of citrus.

Eat for the season. Focus on grains, legumes, and warming root vegetables. Carrots are excellent for digestion, parsnips support the lungs, beets furnish elemental iron, and sweet potatoes are full of vitamins and fiber (and are delicious mashed with butter, cinnamon, and brown sugar!). Try a hot cereal of oatmeal or buckwheat topped with sautéed apples or dried fruit. Enjoy roasted meats, homemade soup stock, and mugs of rich hot chocolate, each with a warming pinch of cayenne. Stewed fruit, crisps, and cobblers make delicious winter treats.

Pamper your body. Enjoy warm baths, adding 1 cup Epsom salts (magnesium sulfate), 1 teaspoon olive oil, and a few drops of essential oil to each tubful. Try lavender for relaxation, or thyme or rosemary for invigoration. If your skin is dry, replace the Epsom salts with colloidal oatmeal (or blend oatmeal to a powder in your food processor). Consider a weekly "spa night" in which you pamper yourself from head to toe.

Feed Your Mind. This is a perfect time to dive into magickal study, work on garb or tool craft, or read the stack of books that's accumulated on the nightstand. Keep a daily journal to track your activities and monitor winter's progress.

Stay active. Engage in slower-paced exercise, such a yoga, Tai Chi, or swimming. Take bundled walks through your neighborhood, watching for seasonal changes.

Serve the tribe. Take care of your own family, but reach out as well. Winter is a powerful time to do volunteer work in your own community.

Celebrate! Honor Yule, Christmas, Imbolc, or whatever holidays sing to you. The winter holidays are the perfect time for lights, gifts, and greenery: be merry and rejoice!

. . . .

Are you ready to hibernate? Honor winter's rhythms and you'll feel the magickal and health benefits that come from slowing down and embracing the season as a restorative time of quiet, rest, and reflection.

Resources

Harlow, John. "Race to Be First to 'Hibernate' Human Beings." *Times On-line*. May 27, 2007. http://www.timesonline.co.uk/tol/news/science/article1845294.ece.

Nesse, Randolphe, and George Williams. *Why We Get Sick. The New Science of Darwinian Medicine*. New York: Vintage, 1996.

Susan Pesznecker's *bio appears on page 56.*

Illustrator: Rik Olson

Magical Ecotourism

Denise Dumars

Call it ecotourism, voluntourism, or whatever you will, it sounds like something that politically correct Yuppies have the time and the money to do before they go back to their armed-response guarded homes in gated-community suburbs, doesn't it? That's what I thought when I first heard those words many years ago. At that point, I never would have imagined I'd be moved to do just that, and do it specifically for "my people"— people who mean something to me because they are my magickal brethren and because a particular place in need,

New Orleans, is part of my family history.

According to the International Ecotourism Society, *ecotourism* is defined as "responsible travel to natural areas that conserves the environment and improves the well-being of local people." And according to New Orleans Online, *voluntourism* is defined as "folks of  all sorts using their vacations and breaks to help those in need."

I know what you're thinking. "But I only get two weeks' vacation a year! I'm tired! I can't spend the whole time scrubbing mold out of houses in the Lower Ninth Ward or picking up clumps of oil on Gulf beaches. Isn't that why we have celebrities to build new houses there? And besides, I don't have the money to travel that far."

I can and will address those concerns. But first, consider your magickal brothers and sisters. It's their environment, too, and as members of what the Religious Tolerance website calls a "neopagan, Earth-centered religion," I think we owe Earth some moppin' up, to say the least. On my trips to New Orleans, I learned that in some ways, the magickal community there was as decimated as the general community, flung to the four elements, if you will. Groundbreaking and important people in occult New Orleans were forced to move away when their homes were destroyed and jobs lost. Some of those who helped define the unique magickal community of the area in books, tarot decks, and with public rituals are now far away. Here's my New Orleans story, as of 2010.

Falling In Love with NOLA

In the summer of 2005, I had already made plans to visit New Orleans (NOLA) during the Christmas season. Then on August 29—five years ago to the day as I write this—Hurricane Katrina made landfall on the Gulf Coast of Louisiana, and the levees that were supposed to save New Orleans from flooding were quickly breached as the hurricane moved inland. Eventually 80 percent of the city would be under water and more than 1,800 people would die.

The rest of the story may be history, but the suffering continues. New wounds were opened on April 20, 2010, when British Petroleum's Deepwater Horizon oil rig exploded, killing eleven workers and spilling millions of gallons of oil into the Gulf of Mexico.

Ecotourism **is defined as "responsible travel to natural areas that conserves the environment and improves the well-being of local people."**

But back in the summer of 2005, my travel plans were shattered and my heart broken. My dream of seeing the city where my father's aunt Josephine had been a nun for sixty-three years, where important people in the magickal community lived, and where some of my ancestors had settled after being expelled from Canada was gone like the levees that were supposed to have kept the flood waters at bay. Here in California, we didn't really know the truth about what was going on or what the long-term effects would be—to some extent, we still don't.

At the time, there was nothing I could do but give money to the fund that Pacific Unitarian Church was collecting for distribution by the UU church in New Orleans (our Iseum holds its seasonal rituals at PUC). As it turned out, I would not travel to New Orleans for the first time until spring 2009. I would return for Yule in 2009 as well.

My first trip to New Orleans was exploratory. Tourism was way down and we were determined to spend our tourist dollars where they were most needed. That meant tours given not by huge companies but by locals; magickal supplies and souvenirs bought at real voodoo and occult shops; food and drinks purchased at historic but not upscale eateries and bars. We walked most of the time, or took the streetcar or bus. We asked a lot of questions. We got a lot of answers, and New Orleans took us in.

There were only five people on the Haunted History Cemetery walking tour that took us through the French Quarter and into St. Louis Cemetery #1, where many noted early residents of New Orleans are buried, including Marie Laveau and some of her family. The tour guide thoughtfully explained how to leave an offering for Mamzelle the proper way, without desecrating the grave as many had done before by marking X's on it with chalk or brick dust. There were plenty of offerings there already: Mardi Gras beads, flowers, candy, gris gris. Most of the above-ground tombs were  in disrepair, some rather startlingly so. The only other sign that anyone had recently visited any of the individuals was the crypt of someone I can only call Mr. Chicken Foot, because his tomb was decorated with some of the familiar chicken-foot based charms one sees in some voodoo shops. A powerful aura of "send back that evil to the one who sent it" came off of his tomb. We were told that the

Catholic archdiocese was in charge of maintaining the cemetery, but it didn't look like anyone had maintained it in a long time.

The French Quarter was virtually the only part of New Orleans spared the worst of the storm. Though it was not yet summer, the heat and humidity were punishing, and even at night the temperature dropped only a little. I was sad to learn that there was no tour available for St. Louis Cemetery #2; it is not a safe cemetery to explore on one's own, so on our next trip we may try to hire a private guide (read: bodyguard). We eschewed the other Haunted History tours, such as the Voodoo tour, as we already knew where to find the real thing.

It is somewhat sad to say that the best-preserved part of old New Orleans actually is the French Quarter, because the Quarter itself is falling apart, sinking into the cypress logs beneath its foundations. I doubt that anyone would be surprised if the corpses of Jean Lafitte,

Marie Laveau, Duke Philippe d'Orleans, and Huey Long all suddenly walked into the Pirates' Alley bar (which is right behind the beautiful St. Louis Cathedral) and ordered an absinthe, a cigarette, and a souvenir T-shirt. After all, that's what I did after attending Christmas mass and lighting a candle for my late Aunt Josephine, or Sister Ignatius as she was known in the order of the Little Sisters of the Poor.

I was determined to meet some real practitioners of Vodou and also to meet some homegrown Pagans. My hometown of Los Angeles is a competitive place that can host heated rivalries among magical groups, so I was unprepared for how often we were made to feel welcomed. On a particularly blistering day, we stumbled into Voodoo Authentica, and my husband promptly fell asleep on the couch in front of the altar for Yemaya. I was a little taken aback, but Brandi, the owner, told me "Oh, yes, I've slept on that couch many times. It's very comfortable."

Voodoo Authentica was not the only place that made us feel at home. On our next trip to NOLA, we were invited not only to an authentic voodoo ceremony but also to the Winter Solstice ritual of the NOLA Merry Meet group of Pagan organizations, which includes a woman named Ty and her group Lamplight Circle. (I got in contact with this organization through a Yahoo group.) It took place by a wonderful street fair on Esplanade. I'd never before eaten Coq au Vin from an open-air booth! We needed to get to the French Quarter afterward and were given a ride there without even having to ask.

Mambo Sallie Ann Glassman of the Island of Salvation Botanica and La Source Ancienne Ounfo had invited me to their ritual, but there are so few flights into New Orleans that I could not get there early enough to attend. Her rituals are open to the public—as long as you participate. As for donations, Sallie Ann says, "money, energy, expertise, and ideas" are all appreciated. She is currently applying for (and getting!) grants to built a much-needed community center/food co-op. After visiting several neighborhoods in New Orleans, my husband and I found a Walgreens on almost every corner. One can buy decent fried chicken and cognac at the local gas stations, but as for full-service grocery stores, well, we couldn't find any.

My second visit to New Orleans, around Yule, had taken on a somber tone due to the death of Theo, a close Iseum friend. I remembered how Theo had literally given someone the shirt off his back on an ecotourism visit to the Yucatan. A worker at his hotel had complimented him on a rather colorful shirt he wore one day, and before he departed for home, he washed it and gave it to the man.

Saving money on our second visit, we stayed at the Canal St. Guest House. It was lovely, but a house behind it lacked a roof and large vines covered it like a Mayan ruin. I saw this frequently, even four and a half years after Katrina: whole neighborhoods of empty foundations and ruins of buildings overgrown with foliage. The airport shuttle would not drive us to our guest house, as it was beyond Claiborne Street. Gang graffiti included voodoo veves. The only post office was miles away. Many of the boutiques of the Garden District, including Leilah Wendell's famous Westgate Necromantic shop, were gone.

Canal Street streetcars had only just started operating again during our Yule trip. There was no streetcar named Desire, but we did take one called Cemeteries, which took us to the City of the Dead at the other end of Canal. I called my co-priestess Lori Nyx from a coffeehouse that had a botanica/marijuana dispensary on one side and the Oddfellows Rest cemetery on the other. "You won't believe where I'm sitting right now," I told her. "I'm having coffee

next to the Santa Muerte statues and sitting close enough to touch someone's headstone." You can't make this stuff up!

Alone, I sat on a bus through Treme to visit Sallie Ann in the Bywater (this was not the Ninth Ward but was Ninth-Ward adjacent); the bus passed through some incredibly poor neighborhoods, and I was depressed. We'd been told not to go to the Lower Ninth Ward alone, to only go on a guided tour, as though it was a war zone. I was too sad to visit the devastated neighborhood on this trip, even to see the nice, shiny celebrity-built houses.

It was threatening rain when I left Sallie Ann's and the temperature was dropping fast, so I called a taxi. I made friends with the driver—one of my Cajun people—and he helped me out several times during my stay, including carrying heavy luggage down flights of stairs and picking me up at the place no airport shuttle would dare to go.

My husband left—ironically for Theo's beloved Yucatan—the day before I did. So on my last day, I saved my money for the reduced-price cab fare my driver promised me and walked all the way to Rampart Street to visit the Voodoo Spiritual Temple again. On our previous trip, my husband, an award-winning photographer, had taken pictures of Priestess Miriam's altars in the temple for free and sent them to her to use in any way she wished. Priestess Miriam's assistant remembered me, and I told her that I wanted to give an offering for my late friend, Theo, on Ellegua's altar, since he had been particularly fond of Ellegua. She agreed, and I followed her through the store and into the private temple out back. She then surprised me by saying that it was quiet, so she was going to let me stay as long as I wanted. She left me alone, and I spent time at every altar, leaving an offering of money and sometimes a petition, lighting candles, talking to the loa, the orishas, the gods.

I cannot wait to go back to New Orleans, and hopefully help to build something for the city, the way the city has already built a home in my heart.

Getting Involved

One can learn a lot from voluntourism and ecotourism websites. On the Volun-Tourism website, I learned that New Age publisher Inner Ocean pairs with the company Brilliant Voices to bring tourists to help conserve the environment and culture of Maui, including its spiritual practices. What a great place to feel good about traveling to! Mainstream travel guides never used to mention magico-religious rites as destinations, and if they did, it was only a listing of re-creations of "native rituals" geared solely toward nonbelieving tourists.

But things have changed! Even the upscale travel magazine *Condé Nast Traveler*, as part of a larger Pico Iyer article on travel to the holy land, inset a companion article that includes such information as how to make contacts to visit Candomblé *terreiros* in Brazil. I can't say I've ever seen this before. *Frommer's New Orleans* guide helped me distinguish ahead of time the voodoo sites that are the real thing and not just tourist traps, and they turned out to be right on the money.

You don't have to be in a movie star's tax bracket to help out, either. Remember those free pictures my husband took? I'm a writer; I can publicize ecotourism—and that's what I'm hoping to do with this piece. What talents do you have to contribute? And anyone at all could get involved with Travelocity voluntouring grants. Travelocity provides opportunities to apply for $5,000 grants for the purpose of "voluntouring." Their very Pagan-looking mascot, the Roaming Gnome, says "Make it Earth Day, Every Day." Search the Internet for similar offers. If you are a student, check with your college to see what grants or internships may be available for funding your stay at an ecotourism or voluntourism location. You might even earn college credit and some work experience in the deal.

Search the Internet for similar offers. If you are a student, check with your college to see what … may be available for funding your stay at an ecotourism or voluntourism location.

As Priestess Sallie Ann Glassman says, "It is the duty of human beings to repair, rebuild and transform the world." We who belong to Earth-centered religions need to get right on it.

Resources

Dougherty, Margot. "Divine Destinations." *Condé Nast Traveler*. September 2010. 78–80.

Herczog, Mary. *Frommer's New Orleans 2009*. Hoboken, NJ: Wiley Publishing, 2009.

International Ecotourism Society. http://www.ecotourism.org/.

Iyer, Pico. "The Magic of Holy Places." *Condé Nast Traveler*. September 2010. 77–78.

New Orleans Tourism Marketing Corporation. "Voluntourism." *New Orleans Online*. http://www.neworleansonline.com/neworleans/voluntourism/index.html.

Ontario Consultants on Religious Tolerance. "World Religions; Neo-pagan Religions." *Religious Tolerance.org*. http://www.religioustolerance.org/witchcra.htm.

Travelocity.com. "Travelocity: Voluntourism." http://www.travelocity.com/TravelForGood/ca-guide.html.

Volun-Tourism International. "Supply Chain: Brilliant Voices, Brilliant Volun-Tourism!" http://www.voluntourism.org/news-supplychain23.htm.

Rev. Denise Dumars, M. A., *is a college English instructor and writer who lives in L.A.'s beautiful South Bay. She holds seasonal rituals with her Fellowship of Isis group, the Iseum of Isis Paedusis, and participates in many Southern California Pagan events. She is currently working on a new nonfiction book and a novel.*

Illustrator: Christa Marquez

Making Space Sacred

Jhenah Telyndru

In the ancient past, our ancestors may have looked with reverent awe out over the primeval landscape and saw the essence of divinity in all things. From the gentle murmur of a life-sustaining spring to the awful destructive energies at work in a hurricane gale, the often-capricious nature of Otherworldly forces revealed themselves in the very fabric of the world. Perhaps these ancestors began leaving offerings of food or intentionally created items in places where these energies were felt to be most powerful—especially beautiful vistas,

strangely shaped stones, or deep foreboding cave mouths that filled them with an unnamable dread. These offerings may have been tokens of thanks for a bounty of food, a successful childbirth, or for surviving another winter. Or perhaps gifts were presented in hopes of keeping malevolent forces at bay, to ensure a positive outcome in the hunt, or to secure rest for the spirits of the departed.

In time, as civilization developed and humanity settled in cities and forged grand empires, people's reverence for the gods and ancestors grew as well. Our forbearers erected megalithic monuments, constructed elaborate temple complexes, and dedicated shrines so sacred that only those who had been ritually prepared could set foot within their boundaries. As before, these places of veneration were built at sites deemed somehow sacred or set apart from the mundane world. Something about them was connected to the realms of the spirit, making it easier for our ancestors to communicate with the Otherworld, both to send their requests and supplications, as well as to receive the will and guidance of the Divine. In many societies, the rites of worship and the need for Divine intervention were so central that nothing could be done without first consulting the oracle of the gods or making a sacrificial offering in hopes that they could win the gods' favor.

These same beliefs and practices played out on a smaller scale as well, where individual households and groups of homesteads dedicated their own sacred spaces, whether at central clan places where seasonal gatherings and regional celebrations could be held, or at an individual's hearthside where tribal and personal ancestors could be supplicated and local gods honored. Over space and time, the divinities and spirits being honored at these large communal centers or personal household shrines have changed name and form, often birthing multi-layered traditions whose ancient roots have become completely absorbed into new belief systems. What remains the same, however, is the continued human need to set aside a special place for prayer, contemplation, and worship.

While the grand cathedrals, temples, and mosques of the world speak volumes about the devotion and collective histories of millions of people across the planet, it is the elegant simplicity of the garden temple and the fireside shrine that is the powerful practice of many Pagans today. As varied in form and purpose as the people who built them, these personal altars and reflections on what makes a space sacred are powerful to contemplate. Is it the bringing together of beautiful and meaningful objects to create an energetic mood? Is it the reverent adornment of an already special outdoor space, acknowledging its spiritual essence and connection to the Divine? Or is it the reflection of what each person does in the space that imbues it with a sense of the sacred—an external manifestation of the seeker's process of unfolding, of discovering their own sacred nature, their own inherent holiness, their own sovereign connection to the Divine?

What follows are some ideas and practices I have found useful in creating sacred space for use in ritual, to support clarity and growth in my own home, and to sanctify the very temple of my body. It is my hope that these will serve as inspiration for your own creative expression of the Divine in your own life, and that these will be powerful companions that bless and sustain you as you journey through your own process of transformation, serving as reminder of your own sacred center and the Old Ones who light the altar fire within us all.

It is the elegant simplicity of the garden temple and the fireside shrine that is the powerful practice of many Pagans today.

Flowing with Holy Waters

From the grand European matrons made of stone and marble found in piazzas and formal estates to their simple and elegant bamboo sisters burbling in Zen gardens, fountains have engaged the imaginations of people across time and around the world. I have always been enchanted by the magic of fountains. How wonderful it was for me when they started producing tabletop fountains for the home!

Aside from their visual beauty and calming sounds of running water, I have found fountains to be a powerful tool for setting the energy of my home. Chosen for their specific properties, I love to position stones and crystals under the flow of the water; this cleanses and charges the stones while also releasing their vibrational signatures into the area. Similarly, adding a few drops of

Chalice Well water or one of my homemade Goddess Elixirs to the fountain circulates those energies around the home, supporting my personal work and adding a sacred influence to my living space.

One important elemental characteristic of water is its ability to hold and magnify whatever intention you bring to it. This makes water a potent ally in your spiritual work, especially when it comes to setting an energetic tone where you live and work. Instead of a fountain, you can charge a bowl of water with a quality you want to bring into your space—perhaps supporting this intention with similarly toned stone, elixir, or essential oil placed in the bowl—and allow it to gently diffuse into the area as the water evaporates. This is a simple way to bring a touch of the sacred to your surroundings, to reinforce your spiritual work, and to empower yourself to be surrounded by positive energies of your own choosing.

Igniting the Sacred Center

Whether it's the central fire pits of the wattle and daub roundhouses of the British Celts or the Eternal Flame that burned in the marble columned austerity of the circular Temple of Vesta in ancient Rome, the power of the hearth has always been at the heart of the human experience. More than a place of warmth, light, and sustenance, the flicker of the hearth fire is a place for families to gather, for stories to be shared, and for collective traditions and memories to be perpetuated.

When purchasing our first house, a fireplace was on my list of must-haves, and it quickly became central to our family life. My spinning wheel sits on the extra-large hearth, which my children have used as a stage for their impromptu performances and as a platform for their drumming sessions. A two-foot-high statue of the Goddess graces the wooden mantle, a comforting reminder of Her overseeing presence. An offering plate and a bowl where I place my

healing requests sit on either side of the statue, which at night is illuminated by pure white pillar candles. I enjoy decorating the mantle with seasonal symbols collected from nature, creating a dynamic and ever-evolving representation of the cycle of the year.

Even if you do not have a fireplace, it can be empowering to choose a place in your home that will hold the energies of the Sacred Center. Perhaps you can use a small side table as a house altar, or set aside a book shelf for symbols and objects that remind you of your life's big picture or that hold the energy of the whole and holy you. The flicker of a consciously chosen candle flame can serve as a proxy for a central hearth fire, while still reflecting the illumination of your spirit's core—bright and warm in its constant connection with the loving energies of the Divine.

Honoring the Great Cycle

Leaving offerings in sacred places is a tradition rooted in the practice of ritual sacrifice. Where once our ancestors made sacrifices to the gods and spirits to ensure a good harvest or to gain Otherworldly protection, today we seek assistance in reaping the bounty of our soul's potential. Taking time to express gratitude to those who support us in our work and witness us in our process—both in this world and in the Otherworld—is an acknowledgement of the greater tapestry of our lives. This balances the give and take of spiritual energies and is a powerful reflection of our soul's growth.

Over the years, I have had the honor and privilege to stand with sisters in sacred space in many different settings—in ancient landscapes, on moonlit beaches, in backyard pavilions, and in lovingly prepared living rooms. One of my favorite ritual sites was a wild apple grove in the middle of a nature preserve. The trees formed a natural circle, and it was incredible to celebrate the Cycle of the Year surrounded by the arms of their changing branches. We left a small ceramic bowl in a niche formed by their wonderfully gnarled roots; each month we would offer the grove the contents of the bowl as thanks for their support in our work.

It was beautiful to see what the elements would offer up: rainwater, most months, sometimes festooned with delicate white and pink blossoms; other times a brown leaf or two would float on its surface. In the drier summer months, the bowl became hidden in the overgrowth of the forest floor, and in the fall, we often had to clear the fallen apples away in order to even find the bowl. It was lovely to pass the bowl around and bless its contents, adding our energy to what nature had already provided. Although we brought libations of wine and cider to share with the area each month, there was something especially fitting in reflecting the blessings of nature back upon itself.

Harnessing the Blessings of Air

I love the sound of chimes playing in the wind, and (much to my neighbors' chagrin at times) I have a small orchestra's worth pealing their song into the night. These chimes make more than beautiful music, however. There is an ancient Celtic tradition of tying prayer ribbons to trees in sacred groves or around holy wells. People would infuse the scraps of cloth with their hopes and needs, and leave them for the wind to carry their intentions to the gods and Spirits of the Land.

Inspired by this, I charge my wind chimes twice a year—at the portal times of *Calan Gaeaf*/Samhain and *Calan Mai*/Beltane—

with the vision of what I hope to manifest during the Dark and Light Halves of the year. The tubular metal bells of the chimes hold the energy nicely, and when they ring I feel the vibration of each note sending out my intentions into the Universe. Also, their music serves as a constant reminder of my work, and each time I hear them I am reminded of the sacred nature of the daily journey and the ways in which creation conspires to help us.

These energies of transformation call us to rise to the challenge of our personal unfolding and release our intentions for change into the world. As we look within our souls seeking self-understanding during the Dark Half, so now we must initiate action to achieve self-fulfillment during the Light Half of the cycle. Setting up our personal space in support of these changes serves to remind us daily that every time we act, the Universe responds in kind. Every ripple we initiate in the pond of our lives expands ever-outward, challenging the boundaries of who we are and opening new spaces for who we can become.

Sanctifying the Temple of the Body

Of all the spaces that surround us, of all the blessings we send out into the world, of all the things we honor and consider sacred, it is often our own bodies that are most in need of honor and celebration. Considered by many to be the vehicle through which our soul experiences the physical world, our bodies are indeed worthy of recognition as the spiritual temples they are. Too frequently we focus on our perceived physical imperfections, forget the miracle of the body's ability to heal itself when we are ailing, or take for granted the fragile balance our bodies need to sustain us, instead choosing to abuse ourselves with excess, deprive ourselves of adequate sleep or nourishing food, and engage in other physically and psychologically damaging behaviors.

For women especially, how we carry ourselves and think about our body is incredibly emotionally charged. We are constantly being bombarded with messages telling us how we are supposed to look and what we are supposed to wear. Women's bodies have been objectified by a culture that has also programmed us to believe they are objects of sin and shame. Reclaiming the sacred nature of our physical form is a service both to our selves and to our sisters—it is a rejection of the old paradigm and a reframing of how women think about themselves on their own terms.

There is a Hermetic Axiom that states: "As above, so below. As within, so without." Our treatment and reverence for our body both reflects upon, and is a reflection of, the spirit that dwells within. How can you bring a sense of the sacred to your physical self? Perhaps you can incorporate a daily routine of self-anointing with oils you have blessed for this purpose and choose to consciously eat wholesome foods to power your body-temple. Indulge in sacred spa days and pamper yourself with a luxurious bath scented with herbs and flowers that stimulate the essence of the Divine within. Wear colors and styles that reflect your personality and make you feel beautiful, rather than feeling like a slave to the trends of fashion. Adorn yourself with stones and symbolic jewelry that serve as reminders of your holy nature. And, perhaps most importantly, support other women in cultivating a sense of the self as sacred: discourage self-deprecating remarks, do not engage in disempowering body behaviors, and praise your sisters and brothers as the beautiful and perfect beings they are.

While it's useful and beneficial to create a physical sacred space, such as a hearth or garden, creating sacred space within yourself may be the best thing you can do for your spirit.

Jhenah Telyndru *has been blessed to walk a Goddess path for more than two decades. She is the founder and Morgen of the Sisterhood of Avalon and serves as Director of the Avalonian Thealogical Seminary. Jhenah is the author of* Avalon Within: A Sacred Journey of Myth, Mystery, and Inner Wisdom *(Llewellyn) and creator of a unique Avalonian Posture System, demonstrated on the instructional DVD* Trancing the Inner Landscape: Avalonian Landscape Postures. *She presents Avalonian intensives and workshops across the United States and facilitates pilgrimages to sacred sites in the British Isles. Jhenah is a postgraduate student at the University of Wales, Lampeter, where she is earning a master's degree in Celtic studies. Visit her online at www.ynysafallon.com.*

Illustrator: Bri Hermanson

The Lunar Calendar

September 2011 to December 2012

SEPTEMBER

S	M	T	W	T	F	S
				1	2	3
4	5	6	7	8	9	10
11	12	13	14	15	16	17
18	19	20	21	22	23	24
25	26	27	28	29	30	

OCTOBER

S	M	T	W	T	F	S
						1
2	3	4	5	6	7	8
9	10	11	12	13	14	15
16	17	18	19	20	21	22
23	24	25	26	27	28	29
30	31					

NOVEMBER

S	M	T	W	T	F	S
		1	2	3	4	5
6	7	8	9	10	11	12
13	14	15	16	17	18	19
20	21	22	23	24	25	26
27	28	29	30			

DECEMBER

S	M	T	W	T	F	S
				1	2	3
4	5	6	7	8	9	10
11	12	13	14	15	16	17
18	19	20	21	22	23	24
25	26	27	28	29	30	31

2012

JANUARY

S	M	T	W	T	F	S
1	2	3	4	5	6	7
8	9	10	11	12	13	14
15	16	17	18	19	20	21
22	23	24	25	26	27	28
29	30	31				

FEBRUARY

S	M	T	W	T	F	S
			1	2	3	4
5	6	7	8	9	10	11
12	13	14	15	16	17	18
19	20	21	22	23	24	25
26	27	28	29			

MARCH

S	M	T	W	T	F	S
				1	2	3
4	5	6	7	8	9	10
11	12	13	14	15	16	17
18	19	20	21	22	23	24
25	26	27	28	29	30	31

APRIL

S	M	T	W	T	F	S
1	2	3	4	5	6	7
8	9	10	11	12	13	14
15	16	17	18	19	20	21
22	23	24	25	26	27	28
29	30					

MAY

S	M	T	W	T	F	S
		1	2	3	4	5
6	7	8	9	10	11	12
13	14	15	16	17	18	19
20	21	22	23	24	25	26
27	28	29	30	31		

JUNE

S	M	T	W	T	F	S
					1	2
3	4	5	6	7	8	9
10	11	12	13	14	15	16
17	18	19	20	21	22	23
24	25	26	27	28	29	30

JULY

S	M	T	W	T	F	S
1	2	3	4	5	6	7
8	9	10	11	12	13	14
15	16	17	18	19	20	21
22	23	24	25	26	27	28
29	30	31				

AUGUST

S	M	T	W	T	F	S
			1	2	3	4
5	6	7	8	9	10	11
12	13	14	15	16	17	18
19	20	21	22	23	24	25
26	27	28	29	30	31	

SEPTEMBER

S	M	T	W	T	F	S
						1
2	3	4	5	6	7	8
9	10	11	12	13	14	15
16	17	18	19	20	21	22
23	24	25	26	27	28	29
30						

OCTOBER

S	M	T	W	T	F	S
	1	2	3	4	5	6
7	8	9	10	11	12	13
14	15	16	17	18	19	20
21	22	23	24	25	26	27
28	29	30	31			

NOVEMBER

S	M	T	W	T	F	S
				1	2	3
4	5	6	7	8	9	10
11	12	13	14	15	16	17
18	19	20	21	22	23	24
25	26	27	28	29	30	

DECEMBER

S	M	T	W	T	F	S
						1
2	3	4	5	6	7	8
9	10	11	12	13	14	15
16	17	18	19	20	21	22
23	24	25	26	27	28	29
30	31					

This year's Witches' Companion *calendar section focuses on activism: ways you can get involved in your community. Making a change in the world can seem like a daunting task, so here we focus on one topic each month, either in your home or in your community. We hope you'll find the cause that resonates with you, so that you can be the change you want to see in the world!* —Nicole Edman, editor

This year marks the twentieth year of September being Organic Harvest Month, as announced by the Organic Trade Association (OTA). Organics are a hot topic in the food world today, especially with the growing popularity of writers like Michael Pollen and Barbara Kingsolver. While the actual nutritional value of organic food is yet to be decisively proved, the environmental advantage can't be ignored: organic production systems replenish and maintain soil fertility, eliminate toxic and persistent chemical pesticides and fertilizers, and build biologically diverse agriculture.

Some people are put off from buying organic produce by higher prices in the supermarket, but the growing farmers' market trade may provide a cheaper source of organic goods: it's estimated that 40–60 percent of farmers at such markets operate organically.

HOW TO GET INVOLVED

The easiest way is the simplest: buy organic produce. To ease the transition, replace just one item per shopping trip with its organic equivalent. You could also look into Community Supported Agriculture (CSA) farms in your area; eating organic produce is convenient when a boxful is delivered to you each week. Visit www.OTA.com/organic_and_ you/15ways.html for more ways to get involved in Organic Harvest Month. Happy eating!

2011
SEPTEMBER

SU	M	TU	W	TH	F	SA
				1	2	3
4	5	6	7	8	9	10
	Labor Day					
11	12 ☺	13	14	15	16	17
	Harvest Moon 5:27 am					
18	19	20	21	22	23	24
					Mabon/ Fall Equinox	
25	26	27 ● 7:09 am	28	29	30	

New and Full Moon dates are shown in Eastern Time. You must adjust
the time (and date) for your time zone.

I remember diving into the world of Huckleberry Finn as a fourth grader (ambitious, yes), but it turns out I may owe those hours of enjoyment to a stubborn library staff: *The Adventures of Huckleberry Finn* was the fifth most frequently challenged book of the 1990s.

Banned Books Week has been celebrated during this time of year since 1982. According to the American Library Association, Banned Books Week "highlights the benefits of free and open access to information while drawing attention to the harms of censorship by spotlighting actual or attempted bannings of book across the United States."

Books are challenged or targeted for banning from parents or other groups for numerous reasons: sexually explicit content, offensive language, material unsuited to age group, violence, homosexuality, anti-family messages, and religious viewpoints are among the most popular. Nearly 70 percent of challenges take place in classrooms or school libraries, with another 24 percent in public libraries. Censorship is a scary slippery slope, and the Supreme Court has upheld the free expression of ideas time and time again. The Library Bill of Rights states that only parents have the right (and responsibility) to restrict a child's access to library resources. To let the library staff do so would be a violation of the First Amendment.

HOW TO GET INVOLVED

Visit www.ala.org and click on "Issues & Advocacy" for more resources, lists of frequently challenged books by year, and some frequently challenged classics. Encourage your local library to celebrate Banned Books Week, if they don't already, and then snuggle yourself up with a banned book and read on!

2011
OCTOBER

SU	M	TU	W	TH	F	SA
						1
2	3	4	5	6	7	8
9	10 Columbus Day (observed)	11 ☺ Blood Moon, 10:06 pm	12	13	14	15
16	17	18	19	20	21	22
23	24	25	26 ● 3:56 pm	27	28	29
30	31 Samhain/ Halloween					

When I get a little money I buy books; and if any is left I buy food and clothes.
~Desiderius Erasmus

Vegetarian, vegan, pescatarian, raw food diet, fruitarianism . . . what does it all mean? November is Vegan Awareness Month, and with an estimated 3.2 percent of U.S. adults (some 7.3 million people) eating a vegetable-based diet and 1 million of them following a vegan lifestyle, it's worth understanding the vegan ideals.

Veganism is a philosophy that shuns the use of animals for food, clothing, or any other product. While some vegans focus solely on the human diet, the larger movement has its roots in animal rights activism in Britain. Donald Watson founded the Vegan Society on November 1, 1944. Vegans not only abstain from animal flesh and animal-derived foods like milk, honey, or eggs, they don't use leather, wool, fur, down, or cosmetics or other products tested on animals. (In contrast, many vegetarians will consume animal-derived products such as milk or cheese.) Veganism is touted as a cruelty-free lifestyle, aimed at bettering the lives of animals, improving human health, and supporting the environment. The animal meat industry produces an estimated 51 percent of worldwide greenhouse gas emissions and is charged with a great deal of water pollution.

HOW TO GET INVOLVED

If you're not quite committed to the vegan lifestyle, try a gentler approach this month by reducing your overall meat consumption. If meat is a must, buy grass-fed beef, free-range chicken, and other products where the animal's quality of life was taken into consideration. Outside the home, ask your cafeteria or local lunch spot to add vegan-friendly options to their menu.

On the non-food front, avoid goods made from leather or fur, and see if you can swap wool items for those made of cotton.

2011
NOVEMBER

SU	M	TU	W	TH	F	SA
		1 *All Saints' Day*	2	3	4	5
6 *DST ends, 2 am*	7	8 *Election Day (general)*	9	10 ☺ *Mourning Moon, 3:16 pm*	11 *Veterans Day*	12
13	14	15	16	17	18	19
20	21	22	23	24 *Thanksgiving Day*	25 ● *1:10 am* *Solar eclipse*	26
27	28	29	30			

There is no sincerer love than the love of food.
~George Bernard Shaw

On December 10, 1948, the General Assembly of the United Nations adopted the Universal Declaration of Human Rights. In the aftermath of World War II, human rights was a topic of vital importance. An 18-member special commission within the UN, led by Eleanor Roosevelt and comprised of members from around the world, spent nearly three years drafting the seemingly simple declaration. When the declaration was complete, the member countries of the United Nations adopted it without dissent.

December 10 now stands as Human Rights Day, and December is Universal Human Rights Month. The declaration is now the most widely translated document in the world.

So what is it? The Universal Declaration of Human Rights is a legally binding document of 30 articles that ensures all people's right to dignity, liberty, privacy, property, fair employment, health, education, religion, and freedom from slavery and persecution. These rights are inherent to all humans, regardless of "race, colour, sex, language, religion, political or other opinion, national or social origin, property, birth or other status." The declaration can be read in its entirety at www.udhr.org.

HOW TO GET INVOLVED

The Franklin and Eleanor Roosevelt Institute's website for the Universal Declaration of Human Rights provides history, resources, a calendar of events, news, and scores of ideas on how to commemorate this month. Go to www.udhr.org and click on "Action" for ways to get involved in human rights causes. Activities are in five categories: Request and Read, Act Locally, Act Nationally or Internationally, Grab a Partner, and Raise Your Voice.

SU	M	TU	W	TH	F	SA
				1	2	3
4	5	6	7	8	9	10 ☺ Lunar eclipse Long Nights Moon, 9:36 am
11	12	13	14	15	16	17
18	19	20	21	22 Yule/ Winter Solstice	23	24 ● 1:06 pm Christmas Eve
25 Christmas Day	26	27	28	29	30	31 New Year's Eve

When you get to the end of your rope, tie a knot in it and hang on.
~Eleanor Roosevelt

Well, the holidays are over and spring is still far off—are you feeling cabin fever yet? Is the stale winter air making you yearn for fresh air? Maybe that's the feeling that inspired Canada to declare the third week in January Non-Smoking Week back in 1977.

The week's activities are coordinated by the Canadian Council on Smoking and Health. Canada has a very strong national smoking ban, both for indoor public spaces and work spaces, including restaurants, bars, and casinos. The United States has no national smoking ban, but as of March 2010, 26 states have some type of public smoking ban, 7 states have bans that do not include adult locations, 6 states have detailed bans, and 11 states have no statewide smoking ban. In addition, many local governments have passed smoking bans for public spaces. And it's no wonder: cigarette smokers are 20 times more likely to develop lung cancer than non-smokers.

HOW TO GET INVOLVED

While occasional tobacco use is common in ritual, dependence on nicotine is an unhealthy addiction. If you are currently a smoker, there are many resources to help you kick the habit; try www.quitnet.net, www.smokefree.gov, or www.quitsmoking.com. The American Lung Association even offers a free online smoking cessation program. Visit www.lungusa.org and click on "Stop Smoking" for more information.

Are you close to a smoker? Visit www.quitguide.com and click "Help Someone Quit" for tips on supporting others trying to quit.

If you're curious what bans are in effect in your area, try a search of "List of Smoking Bans" on Wikipedia for smoking bans by country and links to a list of smoking bans by state.

2012
JANUARY

SU	M	TU	W	TH	F	SA
1 New Year's Day	2	3	4	5	6	7
8	9 ☺ 2:30 am Cold Moon	10	11	12	13	14
15	16 Martin Luther King, Jr. Day	17	18	19	20	21
22	23 ● 2:39 am	24	25	26	27	28
29	30	31				

We are the music-makers
And we are the dreamers of dreams.
~Arthur O'Shaughnessy

Back in 1926, historian Carter G. Woodson started Negro History Week, celebrated in February due to Civil War president Abraham Lincoln's birthday (February 12, 1809) and the birthday of abolitionist author and former slave Frederick Douglass (c. 1818–February 20, 1895). In 1976, the commemoration was expanded to a month but kept in February. In the UK, however, black history is celebrated in October.

The usefulness of Black History Month is now widely debated, with some arguing that black history is American history, and there is no need to separate the two. But remember: if we don't learn from history, we are doomed to repeat it. Just as we study the Holocaust and wars of old, we ought to examine the slave era and civil rights movement in order to avoid such prejudices in the future.

HOW TO GET INVOLVED

Take some time to learn a bit about the slave era and pledge to uphold racial equality in your community in whatever ways you can. Visit www.blackhistory.com for profiles of historymakers and more. Check your local television listings for special programs this month, particularly on channels like History and Biography. Biography's website has timelines, trivia, and (no surprise) biographies of famous abolitionists and equal rights activists at www.biography.com/blackhistory.

Children are the future of society. Talk with your children and see what impressions they've formed of race and racism. You may be surprised what your children think and what they've absorbed from you, the media, and their friends. Racism is learned: be sure it's not what your children are being taught.

2012
FEBRUARY

SU	M	TU	W	TH	F	SA
			1	2	3	4
				Imbolc/ Groundhog Day		
3	6	7 ☻	8	9	10	11
		Quickening Moon, 4:54 pm				
12	13	14	15	16	17	18
		Valentine's Day				
19	20	21 ●	22	23	24	25
		5:35 pm				
	Presidents' Day					
26	27	28	29			
			Leap Day			

*Uncovering what is wrong must always precede
the discovery of what is right.*
~Guy Finley

PISCES

March is Women's History Month in the United States. The first International Women's Day was on March 8, 1911. Congress passed a resolution to recognize Women's History Week in 1981, and the commemoration gained such popularity in many schools that it was expanded to a whole month in 1987.

Though women were not historically allowed to be explorers, teachers, or scholars, intrepid females have played a great part in the story of humankind. From scientists like Madame Curie, who discovered two new elements, to politicians like Great Britain's Prime Minister Margaret Thatcher, women have been studying, inventing, exploring, and leading since the dawn of time—even if they had to do so behind the scenes.

Some instances of discrimination based on sex do still exist, but women in America have come a long way in recent decades. The eighteenth amendment granted women the right to vote in 1920, and the Civil Rights Act of 1964 outlawed discrimination based on sex, among other things.

HOW TO GET INVOLVED

Visit the website of the National Women's History Project at www. nwhp.org to learn more about the unique role women have played in America's history. This organization was founded in 1980 to celebrate women's accomplishments and provide positive role models for young girls.

Girls Explore is another useful tool for learning about adventurous women. The site (www.girls-explore.com) features books, dolls, and biographies of famous women who changed history. Also included are pages of interesting information and links for children, parents, and educators.

2012
MARCH

SU	M	TU	W	TH	F	SA
				1	2	3
4	5	6	7	8 ☺ Storm Moon, 4:39 am	9	10
11 DST begins, 2 am	12	13	14	15	16	17 St. Patrick's Day
18	19	20 Ostara/ Spring Equinox	21	22 ● 10:37 am	23	24
25	26	27	28	29	30	31

All I am I owe to my mother.
~George Washington

April is Community Service Month in the United States. After reading about months that celebrate history, traditionally oppressed groups of people, and health topics, a whole month dedicated to community service may seem somewhat vague. But sometimes, the simplest ideas are the best. According to a study by Volunteering In America (www.volunteeringinamerica.gov), 63.4 million Americans volunteered in 2009, contributing 8.1 billion hours of service.

A 2007 study found that volunteering offers both social and health benefits. Volunteers have lower mortality rates, higher functional abilities, and less depression than nonvolunteers (www.nationalservice.org). Volunteers often feel they receive just as much as they give.

Monetary donations can do a world of good, but some tasks can only be accomplished with hands-on help. Even if you think you don't have much to offer, an open ear and a kind smile may make all the difference to a person in need. Don't have much time, either? Don't worry! Some volunteer options require very short amounts of time or one-time commitments.

HOW TO GET INVOLVED

Maybe you already have some ideas of where to volunteer in your community, but you just haven't taken that step yet—make a pledge this April to actually get out there and sign up! If you don't already have a favorite cause or specialized skill to offer, try www.serve.gov to find opportunities in your area. You can search for openings based on interest, location, and time. You might also try your local library or school, as they almost always need homework helpers.

APRIL

SU	M	TU	W	TH	F	SA
1 All Fools' Day	2	3	4	5	6 ☺ Wind Moon, 3:19 pm	7
8	9	10	11	12	13	14
15	16	17	18	19	20	21 ● 3:18 am
22 Earth Day	23	24	25	26	27	28
29	30					

It is our choices, Harry, that show what we truly are, far more than our abilities.
~Albus Dumbledore (J. K. Rowling)

TAURUS

May brings warm weather and the coming end of school for most American children. But some kids enter the summer months not knowing where they will sleep or eat, or if their parents will be able to care for them. May is National Foster Care Month. The most recent national data from the Child Welfare Information Gateway (www.childwelfare.gov/fostercaremonth) was collected on September 30, 2008, estimating that there were 463,000 children in out-of-home care at that time. About a quarter of those lived with relatives, but close to half were living in nonrelative foster family homes. Almost half of all foster children remain in the system for less than a year, highlighting the ongoing need for responsible, short-term care. Some children are placed in out-of-home care only until their original family can work through a difficult time or situation, such as chemical dependence, financial straits, or health problems. Being reunited with biological parents or family is the goal in about half of all foster care cases.

HOW TO GET INVOLVED

Interested in becoming a foster family? Visit the National Foster Parent Association at www.nfpainc.org to learn more about the challenges and rewards of foster parenting. Older individuals can volunteer to be foster grandparents through Senior Corps (www.seniorcorps. gov, click on "Foster Grandparents" under the Senior Corps Programs heading).

Those who aren't able or interested in providing foster care can still help children in need. Go to www.fostercaremonth.org and click on the "Change a Lifetime" link (under Get Involved). Here you can find other ways to support the foster care system, whether you have a few weeks, a few hours, or just a few minutes.

2012
MAY

SU	M	TU	W	TH	F	SA
		1	2	3	4	5 ☺
		Beltane				Flower Moon, 11:35 pm
6	7	8	9	10	11	12
13	14	15	16	17	18	19
Mother's Day						
20 ● 7:47 pm	21	22	23	24	25	26
Solar eclipse						
27	28	29	30	31		
	Memorial Day (observed)					

We're all very ordinary in St. Mary Mead,
but ordinary people can do the most astonishing things.
~Miss Marple (Agatha Christie)

June is probably the second-most recognizable monthly topic in this section: Gay and Lesbian Pride Month. (See October 2012 for the most publicized month dedication.) The commemoration was first declared in 2000 by President Clinton. June was chosen in remembrance of the 1969 Stonewall riots that followed a police raid at a gay bar in New York City, which many consider the starting point of the LGBT rights movement. In June 2010, President Obama expanded the designation to Lesbian, Gay, Bisexual, and Transgender Pride Month. That same year saw the repeal of the Don't Ask, Don't Tell rule for gays serving in the US military.

Legislation against hate crimes in general has made great strides in recent years. Leaders of the gay community, as well as celebrities both gay and straight, are now reaching out to LGBT youth to offer support and hope in the face of prejudice.

Another ongoing hot-button issue for the LGBT community is gay marriage. As of this writing, gay "marriage" is legal in ten countries and five US states: Argentina, Belgium, Canada, Iceland, the Netherlands (which was first in 2001), Norway, Sweden, South Africa, Spain, and Sweden; and Connecticut, Iowa, Massachusetts, New Hampshire, and Vermont, as well as the District of Columbia. Many more states and countries recognize "civil unions" between same-sex partners; however, groups continue to push for equal marriage rights for all, regardless of gender.

HOW TO GET INVOLVED

Most cities in the Unites States host Gay Pride festivals, parades, parties, and picnics during June to celebrate diversity and tolerance. Do a simple Internet search combining "Gay Pride" and your city name to find fun and meaningful events and activities of all kinds.

2012
JUNE

SU	M	TU	W	TH	F	SA
					1	2
3	4 ☺	5	6	7	8	9
	Lunar Eclipse Strong Sun Moon, 7:12 am					
10	11	12	13	14	15	16
				Flag Day		
17	18	19 ● 11:02 am	20	21	22	23
Father's Day			Litha/ Summer Solstice			
24	25	26	27	28	29	30

Be who you are and say what you feel,
because those who mind don't matter and those who matter don't mind.
~Dr. Seuss (Theodor Seuss Geisel)

CANCER

In most parts of the Northern Hemisphere, July is the best month to get out and enjoy Mother Nature—which is probably why July is Recreation and Parks Month. Did you know that the United States has 393 national parks, hosting 275 million visitors each year? Yellowstone in Wyoming was the first national park, designated by President Grant in 1872. The National Park Service also maintains other landmarks and heritage areas to preserve our natural and national history. The first state park was Yosemite in California (now a national park), designated by President Lincoln in 1864. All fifty states have state parks, and most require just a low-cost vehicle permit for entry. (Fishing and hunting require separate permits.)

<u>HOW TO GET INVOLVED</u>

Visit www.nps.gov to find national parks nearby or for vacationing. You can camp at many state parks for around $25 per night, per group. Most parks offer showers and flushable toilets these days. If you don't like roughing it, visit your state's DNR website to find parks with cabins or other amenities. Camping at state and national parks is a great way to enjoy nature and give back to sustaining natural spaces at the same time. It can also make for an affordable vacation or staycation for an entire family.

An even easier way to enjoy parks is to visit a local park. Try doing a Google Maps search of your address, then zoom out on the map screen to find green areas. You can volunteer to clean up a local park, whether through an organization or by picking up trash as you see it. You could organize a group to clean up or otherwise improve a local park, or donate play equipment or gardening supplies and expertise. Can't find a park near you? Contact your city government to establish one! Enjoy the sunshine!

2012
JULY

SU	M	TU	W	TH	F	SA
1	2	3 ☺ Blessing Moon, 2:52 pm	4 Independence Day	5	6	7
8	9	10	11	12	13	14
15	16	17	18	19 ● 12:24 am	20	21
22	23	24	25	26	27	28
29	30	31				

The emotional appeal of nature is tremendous,
sometimes almost more than one can bear.
~Jan Smuts

The sun beating down on your shoulders, car seats and steering wheels too hot to touch, heat radiating up from the sidewalk in visible waves...thirsty yet? August is National Water Quality Month in the United States. While Earth is two-thirds water, most of that is salt water, which is not drinkable without treatment. The average person requires 25–50 liters of clean, safe water each day for drinking, cooking, and cleaning, according to www.drinkingwater. org. Nearly 1 billion people lack access to safe drinking water. That's one in six humans! Unsafe water can be the cause of many diseases and sicknesses. A lack of clean water also makes growing and producing food much more difficult, contributing to hunger problems.

In the United States, water suppliers are subject to the Safe Drinking Water Act. Passed by Congress in 1974 and enforced by the Environmental Protection Agency (EPA), this act requires that drinking water be clear of harmful organisms and chemical pollution. Each year in July, water suppliers are required to send water quality reports to residents. If a supplier serves more than 100,000 people, the report must be made available online.

HOW TO GET INVOLVED

Visit www.epa.gov and click the "Info Where You Live" map to find out if your area's water quality report is available online. You can also click on the "Drinking Water" link on the left side of the page for more information. Learn which minerals are in your water and their effect on the human body.

There are many relief organizations that need your help to improve water quality and access in developing parts of the world. Try www.water.org, www.h2oafrica.org, or thewaterproject.org.

2012
AUGUST

SU	M	TU	W	TH	F	SA
			1 ☺ Corn Moon, 11:27 pm Lammas	2	3	4
5	6	7	8	9	10	11
12	13	14	15	16	17 ● 11:54 am	18
19	20	21	22	24	25	26
27	28	29 ☺ Blue Moon, 9:58 am	30	31		

The cure for anything is salt water—sweat, tears, or the sea.
~Isak Dinesn

VIRGO

It's a common misconception that Cinco de Mayo is the Mexican independence day. That day is actually September 16, which is part of the reason Hispanic Heritage Month runs from September 15 to October 15. September 15 is the national independence day for Costa Rica, El Salvador, Guatemala, Honduras, and Nicaragua. Chile's independence day is September 18. The commemoration started as a week in 1968 under President Johnson. President Reagan expanded the celebration to a month in 1988. Hispanic Heritage Month is meant to celebrate and honor those Americans with ancestry in Spain, Mexico, the Caribbean, and Central and South America. These peoples played a major role in America's founding and early history, particularly in western and southern states. Today, there are many famous Hispanic Americans in government, entertainment, and the business world.

It will come as no surprise to many that Spanish is America's second most common language, behind English. The Census Bureau estimated in 2009 that there were 45 million Hispanics in the United States, with 35.5 million people speaking Spanish in the home. Spanish is also the most common second language in America.

HOW TO GET INVOLVED

Visit www.hispanicheritagemonth.gov for lots more information about this month of celebration. For biographies, trivia, and videos, visit www.biography.com/hispanic-heritage. If you have young ones in your life, Scholastic has a great page of information and activities at http://teacher.scholastic.com/activities/hispanic. The page includes history, famous Latinos, games, and even a section called My Heritage for children of Hispanic descent.

2012
SEPTEMBER

SU	M	TU	W	TH	F	SA
						1
2	3 *Labor Day*	4	5	6	7	8
9	10	11	12	13	14	15 ● 10:11 pm
16	17	18	19	20	21 UN International Day of Peace	22 Mabon/ Fall Equinox
23	24	25	26	27	28	29 ☺ Harvest Moon, 11:19 pm
30						

Leaves and stems weave in hymns of light
in the last glow of September sunset and dusk.
~"Weeds" H. Arnett

We now come to our most famous monthly commemoration: National Breast Cancer Awareness Month (NBCAM). Every year in October, the color pink appears everywhere from coffee shops to the fields of the National Football League, raising awareness of the second most prevalent cancer in US females. Each year about 200,000 new cases of invasive breast cancer are diagnosed in the United States, and about 40,000 women will die from the disease. The numbers of cases have risen dramatically in recent decades, but thanks to research advances and early detection methods, the overall mortality rate has actually dropped.

NBCAM began in 1985 as a week-long dedication to educating people about breast cancer. Today the organization is a partnership of health and government agencies and public service groups that try to promote awareness of the disease, share information and support, and provide screening access. Many people's awareness of breast cancer causes is based on charity and fund-raising efforts. Among these are the National Race for the Cure, the Breast Cancer 2 Day, the Breast Cancer 3 Day For the Cure, the Ride to Empower, Global Illumination (lighting buildings in pink), Pink Comic Strips, and various Pink Days.

HOW TO GET INVOLVED

Early detection is the best way to fight breast cancer, so ask a friend to be your screening buddy. Pick a day and email or call each other each month to remind yourselves to do your self breast exam. Even if you are young, self exams are a great way to establish a baseline, so you'll notice even minor changes down the road. Visit www.nbcam .org for information on patient support, breast cancer news, disease facts, events, and their great section on "How to Help."

2012
OCTOBER

SU	M	TU	W	TH	F	SA
	1	2	3	4	5	6
7	8 Columbus Day (observed)	9	10	11	12	13
14	15 ● 8:02 am	16	17	18	19	20
21	22	23	24	25	26	27
28	29 ☺ Blood Moon, 3:49 pm	30	31 Samhain/ Halloween			

Beauty is how you feel inside, and it reflects in your eye.
It is not something physical.
~Lauren Bacall

SCORPIO

As we enter winter our minds turn to the coming holidays. Feasting is a big part of both Thanksgiving and Christmas, and many of us put on a few "holiday pounds" before the end of the year. Perhaps that is why November is Good Nutrition Month. Begun in 1973 with the theme "Invest in Yourself—Buy Nutrition," this is a month to reevaluate your food choices and make changes for the better. Nutrition education is making great strides in America, thanks in part to movies like *Food, Inc.* and *SuperSize Me.* But the fact remains that we must educate ourselves on good eating practices in order to maintain a healthy weight and strong body and mind.

The holidays are also a crucial time for food banks and hunger-relief charities. According to Feeding America, one in six Americans doesn't have access to enough healthy food. That's 49 million Americans, including 14 million children. Part of the nutrition/hunger problem is that the cheapest foods are often the least nutritious for our bodies. When you have only a few dollars to spend, getting an entire meal for $2 is much more attractive than buying a small amount of fresh produce or lean meat. Keep nutrition in mind as you donate to your local hunger-relief charities this season.

HOW TO GET INVOLVED

Visit www.nutrition.gov or www.mypyramid.gov for helpful nutrition guidelines from the US Department of Agriculture. Here you can find your personal recommendations for grains, vegetables, fruits, dairy, meat, and oil consumption, based on your age and sex. Print a pyramid this month and write in your suggested servings (be sure to look up what counts as a serving first). Then dedicate one week to meeting those goals every day and see how you feel. You might be surprised what just one week of good nutrition will do!

2012
NOVEMBER

SU	M	TU	W	TH	F	SA
				1 *All Saints' Day*	2	3
4 *DST ends, 2 am*	5	6 *Election Day (general)*	7	8	9	10
11 *Veterans Day*	12	13 ● *5:08 pm* *Solar eclipse*	14	15	16	17
18	19	20	21	22 *Thanksgiving Day*	23	24
25	26	27	28 ☺ *Lunar eclipse Mourning Moon, 9:46 am*	29	30	

Choose food that is as beautiful as you wish to be yourself.
~Victoria Moran

If October is a month of pink ribbons, December is a month of red ribbons. Red ribbons are meant to commemorate AIDS awareness, and December is AIDS Awareness Month in America. World AIDS Day was set as December 1 in 1987 by two officers at the Global Programme on Aids (part of the World Health Organization). Why December 1? The officials felt that the post-election, pre-Christmas weeks were a slow news time—their day would likely get more media coverage than at another time of year. Today World AIDS Day and AIDS Awareness Month are time to raise awareness about the pandemic of AIDS/HIV and to remember those who have lost their lives to the virus.

Acquired immunodeficiency syndrome (AIDS) and human immunodeficiency virus (HIV) were first recognized by the Centers for Disease Control in 1981. Since that time, more than 25 million people have lost their lives. HIV is sexually transmitted or blood transmitted. It is a virus that weakens the body's defenses and leaves it vulnerable to other sicknesses, which then cause death. The AIDS pandemic supposedly began in Africa, and that is where the disease still hits hardest, claiming ¾ of AIDS deaths. A person can live with the virus for years before becoming ill enough to be diagnosed with full-blown AIDS; then their survival time is about nine months.

HOW TO GET INVOLVED

There is no known cure for AIDS, and misinformation about transmission abounds. Visit www.aids.gov and take time to educate yourself about the disease and the latest news. The website also includes resources for patients and event ideas, as well as suggestions for individual action. Above all, be safe about sex and all forms of bodily fluid contact.

DECEMBER

SU	M	TU	W	TH	F	SA
						1
2	3	4	5	6	7	8
9	10	11	12	13 ● 3:42 am	14	15
16	17	18	19	20	21 Yule/ Winter Solstice	22
23	24 Christmas Eve	25 Christmas Day	26	27	28 ☺ Long Night's Moon, 5:21 am	29
30	31 New Year's Eve					

The greatest things ever done on Earth have been done little by little.
~William Jennings Bryan

Moon Void-of-Course Data for 2011

Last Aspect Date Time	New Sign Sign New Time

JANUARY

Last Aspect	New Sign
2 9:08 a	3 ♑ 2:39 a
5 7:15 a	5 ♒ 11:08 a
7 3:51 p	7 ♓ 9:57 p
10 6:12 a	10 ♈ 10:24 a
12 9:47 p	12 ♉ 10:37 p
15 7:47 a	15 ♊ 8:23 a
17 12:57 p	17 ♋ 2:29 p
19 4:26 p	19 ♌ 5:16 p
21 1:57 p	21 ♍ 6:10 p
23 3:08 p	23 ♎ 6:59 p
25 5:04 p	25 ♏ 9:15 p
27 10:01 p	28 ♐ 1:55 a
30 5:10 a	30 ♑ 9:04 a

FEBRUARY

Last Aspect	New Sign
1 2:32 p	1 ♒ 6:21 p
4 1:11 a	4 ♓ 5:24 a
6 2:13 p	6 ♈ 5:45 p
9 2:31 a	9 ♉ 6:22 a
11 2:27 p	11 ♊ 5:20 p
13 10:19 p	14 ♋ 12:48 a
16 2:06 a	16 ♌ 4:14 a
18 3:36 a	18 ♍ 4:39 a
20 2:18 a	20 ♎ 4:01 a
22 3:35 a	22 ♏ 4:29 a
24 6:14 a	24 ♐ 7:46 a
26 1:08 p	26 ♑ 2:32 p
28 11:03 p	3/1 ♒ 12:14 a

MARCH

Last Aspect	New Sign
2/28 11:03 p	1 ♒ 12:14 a
3 9:36 a	3 ♓ 11:47 a
5 11:34 p	6 ♈ 12:14 a
8 11:04 a	8 ♉ 12:52 p
11 12:26 a	11 ♊ 12:31 a
13 9:10 a	13 ♋ 10:29 a
15 6:05 a	15 ♌ 3:33 p
17 3:58 p	17 ♍ 4:53 p
19 2:10 p	19 ♎ 4:03 p
21 2:35 p	21 ♏ 3:17 p
23 4:08 p	23 ♐ 4:45 p
25 9:25 p	25 ♑ 9:57 p
27 11:17 p	28 ♒ 7:00 a
30 6:21 p	30 ♓ 6:38 p
31 9:44 a	4/2 ♈ 7:16 a

APRIL

Last Aspect	New Sign
3/31 9:44 a	2 ♈ 7:16 a
4 6:04 a	4 ♉ 7:46 p
5 7:02 p	7 ♊ 7:22 a
8 10:24 p	9 ♋ 5:02 p
11 8:05 a	11 ♌ 11:37 p
13 3:58 p	14 ♍ 2:40 a
15 4:49 p	16 ♎ 2:59 a
17 10:44 p	18 ♏ 2:19 a
20 12:53 a	20 ♐ 2:50 a
21 12:57 p	22 ♑ 6:24 a
23 8:13 p	24 ♒ 1:59 p
26 7:28 a	27 ♓ 12:57 a
27 3:53 p	29 ♈ 1:33 p

MAY

Last Aspect	New Sign
1 11:20 a	2 ♉ 1:58 a
3 2:51 a	4 ♊ 1:09 p
6 4:12 p	6 ♋ 10:32 p
9 2:52 a	9 ♌ 5:35 a
11 12:52 a	11 ♍ 9:59 a
12 10:52 p	13 ♎ 11:56 p
15 12:01 p	15 ♏ 12:31 p
17 7:09 a	17 ♐ 1:22 p
19 10:17 a	19 ♑ 4:16 p
21 5:04 p	21 ♒ 10:32 p
24 3:40 a	24 ♓ 8:24 a
25 2:15 p	26 ♈ 8:36 p
29 6:28 a	29 ♉ 9:02 a
31 11:37 a	31 ♊ 7:56 p

JUNE

Last Aspect	New Sign
3 4:08 a	3 ♋ 4:36 a
5 1:33 a	5 ♌ 11:03 a
7 11:27 a	7 ♍ 3:33 p
9 4:13 a	9 ♎ 6:31 p
11 4:04 a	11 ♏ 8:33 p
13 1:43 p	13 ♐ 10:38 p
15 11:31 p	16 ♑ 1:59 a
18 4:07 a	18 ♒ 7:47 a
20 4:23 p	20 ♓ 4:45 p
21 10:51 p	23 ♈ 4:24 a
24 6:07 p	25 ♉ 4:53 p
27 12:24 p	27 ♊ 3:56 a
30 3:33 a	30 ♋ 12:13 p

JULY

Last Aspect	New Sign
1 7:37 a	2 ♌ 5:43 p
3 12:25 p	4 ♍ 9:15 p
5 8:19 p	6 ♎ 11:54 p
8 2:29 a	9 ♏ 2:31 a
10 9:05 a	11 ♐ 5:47 a
12 8:21 a	13 ♑ 10:14 a
15 2:40 a	15 ♒ 4:30 p
17 8:23 a	18 ♓ 1:13 a
20 7:15 a	20 ♈ 12:25 p
22 5:34 p	23 ♉ 12:58 a
25 9:12 a	25 ♊ 12:34 p
27 8:35 p	27 ♋ 9:11 p
28 7:03 p	30 ♌ 2:16 a

AUGUST

Last Aspect	New Sign
1 2:20 a	1 ♍ 4:41 a
1 7:38 a	3 ♎ 6:04 a
5 7:56 a	5 ♏ 7:57 a
7 11:14 a	7 ♐ 11:21 a
9 4:24 p	9 ♑ 4:38 p
10 4:34 p	11 ♒ 11:47 p
14 8:25 a	14 ♓ 8:54 a
15 4:21 a	16 ♈ 8:01 p
19 7:50 a	19 ♉ 8:36 a
21 7:59 p	21 ♊ 8:53 p
24 5:33 a	24 ♋ 6:31 a
25 9:04 a	26 ♌ 12:09 p
28 1:11 p	28 ♍ 2:13 p
29 6:15 p	30 ♎ 2:25 p

SEPTEMBER

Last Aspect	New Sign
1 1:35 p	1 ♏ 2:48 p
3 3:41 p	3 ♐ 5:03 p
5 8:30 p	5 ♑ 10:03 p
7 4:35 p	8 ♒ 5:42 a
10 1:32 p	10 ♓ 3:26 p
12 9:45 p	13 ♈ 2:49 a
15 1:10 p	15 ♉ 3:25 p
18 3:09 a	18 ♊ 4:06 a
20 12:33 p	20 ♋ 2:53 p
22 9:22 p	22 ♌ 9:55 p
24 10:39 p	25 ♍ 12:49 a
25 3:47 p	27 ♎ 12:51 a
28 9:51 p	29 ♏ 12:05 a
30 10:17 p	10/1 ♐ 12:42 a

OCTOBER

Last Aspect	New Sign
9/30 10:17 p	1 ♐ 12:42 a
3 1:37 a	3 ♑ 4:16 a
5 1:58 a	5 ♒ 11:18 a
7 6:08 p	7 ♓ 9:13 p
8 12:51 p	10 ♈ 8:57 a
12 8:08 p	12 ♉ 9:35 p
15 6:51 a	15 ♊ 10:15 a
17 6:18 p	17 ♋ 9:38 p
19 11:30 p	20 ♌ 6:06 a
22 8:34 a	22 ♍ 10:40 a
23 4:47 p	24 ♎ 11:49 a
26 8:18 a	26 ♏ 11:08 a
28 7:49 a	28 ♐ 10:45 a
30 9:30 a	30 ♑ 12:39 p

NOVEMBER

Last Aspect	New Sign
1 5:00 p	1 ♒ 6:08 p
3 11:40 p	4 ♓ 3:18 a
5 4:05 a	6 ♈ 2:02 p
9 12:46 a	9 ♉ 2:45 a
11 11:27 a	11 ♊ 3:10 p
13 10:42 p	14 ♋ 2:19 a
16 12:22 a	16 ♌ 11:17 a
18 2:05 p	18 ♍ 5:19 p
20 5:21 p	20 ♎ 8:16 p
22 6:04 p	22 ♏ 8:58 p
24 6:04 p	24 ♐ 8:57 p
26 7:06 p	26 ♑ 10:05 p
28 6:01 p	29 ♒ 2:02 a

DECEMBER

Last Aspect	New Sign
1 6:27 a	1 ♓ 9:45 a
2 1:06 p	3 ♈ 8:51 p
6 6:13 a	6 ♉ 9:34 a
8 6:39 p	8 ♊ 9:52 p
11 5:24 a	11 ♋ 8:26 a
13 11:05 a	13 ♌ 4:48 p
15 8:20 p	15 ♍ 10:58 p
17 9:29 p	18 ♎ 3:06 a
20 4:49 a	20 ♏ 5:33 a
22 4:49 a	22 ♐ 7:03 a
24 6:36 a	24 ♑ 8:47 a
26 8:36 a	26 ♒ 12:14 p
28 4:31 p	28 ♓ 6:45 p
30 8:37 a	31 ♈ 4:48 a

Moon Void-of-Course Data for 2012

Last Aspect Date	Time	New Sign Sign	New Time
JANUARY			
2	3:07 p	2 ♉	5:16 p
5	3:46 a	5 ♊	5:44 a
7	2:52 p	7 ♋	4:05 p
9	9:25 p	9 ♌	11:35 p
12	3:23 a	12 ♍	4:44 a
13	8:58 p	14 ♎	8:28 a
16	10:29 a	16 ♏	11:33 a
18	1:31 p	18 ♐	2:29 p
20	4:49 p	20 ♑	5:40 p
22	8:38 p	22 ♒	9:53 p
25	3:33 a	25 ♓	4:11 a
26	11:53 p	27 ♈	1:28 p
30	1:08 a	30 ♉	1:28 a
FEBRUARY			
1	2:06 p	1 ♊	2:14 p
4	12:06 a	4 ♋	1:04 a
6	7:31 a	6 ♌	8:24 a
8	11:42 a	8 ♍	12:32 p
10	12:11 a	10 ♎	2:54 p
12	4:09 p	12 ♏	5:01 p
14	12:04 p	14 ♐	7:56 p
16	11:03 p	17 ♑	12:03 a
19	4:22 a	19 ♒	5:28 a
21	11:17 a	21 ♓	12:31 p
22	9:24 p	23 ♈	9:48 p
26	7:52 a	26 ♉	9:29 a
28	2:46 p	28 ♊	10:27 p
MARCH			
2	8:14 a	2 ♋	10:08 a
4	5:17 p	4 ♌	6:17 p
6	8:27 p	6 ♍	10:35 p
8	4:39 a	8 ♎	11:50 p
10	10:09 a	11 ♏	12:24 a
12	2:30 p	13 ♐	2:54 a
15	3:34 a	15 ♑	6:24 a
17	9:00 a	17 ♒	12:11 p
19	4:31 p	19 ♓	8:05 p
21	4:39 a	22 ♈	5:57 a
24	1:17 p	24 ♉	5:43 p
27	12:35 a	27 ♊	6:43 a
29	2:05 p	29 ♋	7:07 p
APRIL			
1	12:20 a	1 ♌	4:35 a
3	9:47 a	3 ♍	9:53 a
5	1:37 a	5 ♎	11:32 a
7	6:15 a	7 ♏	11:18 a
9	2:56 a	9 ♐	11:12 a
11	7:06 a	11 ♑	1:02 p
13	1:05 p	13 ♒	5:48 p
15	6:42 p	16 ♓	1:38 a
17	10:34 a	18 ♈	11:59 a
20	3:35 p	21 ♉	12:05 a
22	1:10 p	23 ♊	1:05 p
25	4:31 p	26 ♋	1:42 a
28	3:05 a	28 ♌	12:10 p
30	10:17 a	30 ♍	7:02 p

Last Aspect Date	Time	New Sign Sign	New Time
MAY			
2	6:58 a	2 ♎	10:04 p
4	2:02 p	4 ♏	10:20 p
6	8:14 a	6 ♐	9:39 p
8	9:34 p	8 ♑	10:00 p
10	3:11 p	11 ♒	1:03 a
12	8:52 p	13 ♓	7:42 a
15	7:59 a	15 ♈	5:45 p
17	5:44 p	18 ♉	6:03 a
20	8:35 a	20 ♊	7:05 p
22	6:51 p	23 ♋	7:31 a
25	10:34 a	25 ♌	6:11 p
27	7:54 p	28 ♍	2:06 a
30	1:50 a	30 ♎	6:46 a
31	9:31 p	4/1 ♏	8:31 a
JUNE			
3/31	9:31 p	1 ♏	8:31 a
3	5:29 a	3 ♐	8:32 a
5	1:08 a	5 ♑	8:31 a
7	8:38 a	7 ♒	10:17 a
9	2:33 p	9 ♓	3:22 p
11	6:41 a	12 ♈	12:21 a
13	11:09 p	14 ♉	12:22 p
16	8:09 a	17 ♊	1:24 a
19	11:02 a	19 ♋	1:34 p
21	12:48 p	21 ♌	11:47 p
23	6:26 p	24 ♍	7:42 a
26	6:53 a	26 ♎	1:15 p
28	4:22 a	28 ♏	4:32 p
30	3:46 p	30 ♐	6:04 p
JULY			
2	6:21 p	2 ♑	6:51 p
4	8:25 a	4 ♒	8:26 p
6	11:49 a	7 ♓	12:29 a
8	7:00 a	9 ♈	8:14 a
11	5:23 a	11 ♉	7:30 p
13	3:46 p	14 ♊	8:26 a
16	6:56 a	16 ♋	8:31 p
19	12:24 a	19 ♌	6:13 a
21	1:17 a	21 ♍	1:24 p
22	8:44 p	23 ♎	6:38 p
25	11:22 a	25 ♏	10:29 p
26	11:38 a	28 ♐	1:18 a
29	5:01 p	30 ♑	3:29 a
31	7:30 p	8/1 ♒	5:56 a
AUGUST			
7/31	7:30 p	1 ♒	5:56 a
3	3:24 a	3 ♓	9:58 a
5	1:56 p	5 ♈	4:59 p
7	4:04 p	8 ♉	3:28 a
9	2:55 p	10 ♊	4:11 p
12	5:49 p	13 ♋	4:27 a
15	4:21 a	15 ♌	2:05 p
17	1:55 p	17 ♍	8:33 p
18	7:26 p	20 ♎	12:45 a
22	3:13 a	22 ♏	3:54 a
23	5:34 a	24 ♐	6:50 p
26	2:39 a	26 ♑	9:58 a
28	6:33 a	28 ♒	1:38 p
30	1:48 p	30 ♓	6:31 p

Last Aspect Date	Time	New Sign Sign	New Time
SEPTEMBER			
1	4:02 p	2 ♈	1:37 a
4	7:06 a	4 ♉	11:41 a
5	2:54 p	7 ♊	12:10 a
9	6:59 a	9 ♋	12:49 p
11	5:58 p	11 ♌	11:00 p
14	1:14 a	14 ♍	5:30 a
16	7:26 a	16 ♎	8:55 a
18	7:30 a	18 ♏	10:46 a
20	9:11 a	20 ♐	12:34 p
22	12:45 p	22 ♑	3:20 p
24	5:19 p	24 ♒	7:32 p
26	11:33 p	27 ♓	1:23 a
28	10:35 p	29 ♈	9:14 a
OCTOBER			
1	6:32 p	1 ♉	7:26 p
3	3:44 a	4 ♊	7:47 a
5	5:08 p	6 ♋	8:45 p
8	3:33 a	9 ♌	7:55 a
10	5:40 p	11 ♍	3:23 p
12	7:48 p	13 ♎	7:02 p
15	8:02 a	15 ♏	8:06 p
16	10:23 p	17 ♐	8:26 p
19	4:27 p	19 ♑	9:41 p
21	11:32 p	22 ♒	1:02 a
23	9:27 p	24 ♓	7:00 a
26	11:04 a	26 ♈	3:31 p
27	9:32 p	29 ♉	2:15 a
29	5:01 p	31 ♊	2:40 p
NOVEMBER			
2	5:21 a	3 ♋	3:43 a
4	3:37 a	5 ♌	2:39 p
7	10:27 a	7 ♍	11:35 p
9	7:27 p	10 ♎	4:35 a
12	12:13 a	12 ♏	6:10 a
14	5:39 a	14 ♐	5:52 a
16	4:44 a	16 ♑	5:35 a
18	12:54 a	18 ♒	7:10 a
20	9:31 a	20 ♓	11:55 a
22	1:32 a	22 ♈	8:12 p
23	8:34 p	25 ♉	7:18 a
26	7:57 p	27 ♊	7:58 p
28	8:04 p	30 ♋	8:55 a
DECEMBER			
2	1:55 a	2 ♌	8:57 p
4	5:08 p	5 ♍	6:51 a
7	5:35 a	7 ♎	1:35 p
8	7:37 p	9 ♏	4:51 p
11	8:08 a	11 ♐	5:22 p
13	3:42 a	13 ♑	4:43 p
15	4:15 p	15 ♒	4:53 p
17	1:12 p	17 ♓	7:48 p
20	12:19 a	20 ♈	2:43 a
22	7:57 a	22 ♉	1:25 p
25	12:58 a	25 ♊	2:13 a
27	1:50 a	27 ♋	3:06 p
28	9:43 a	30 ♌	2:45 a
31	4:52 p	1/1 ♍	4:48 a

Notes:

Notes:

Notes:

Notes: